WITH PEN AND VOICE

A CRITICAL ANTHOLOGY
OF NINETEENTH-CENTURY
AFRICAN-AMERICAN WOMEN

Edited with an Introduction by
SHIRLEY WILSON LOGAN

SOUTHERN ILLINOIS UNIVERSITY PRESS
CARBONDALE AND EDWARDSVILLE

98 97 96 95   4 3 2 1

Library of Congress Cataloging-in-Publication Data

With pen and voice : a critical anthology of nineteenth-century African-
  American women / edited with an introduction by Shirley Wilson Logan.
      p.   cm.
    Includes bibliographical references (p.   ) and index.
    1. Speeches, addresses, etc., American—Afro-American authors.
  2. Speeches, addresses, etc., American—Women authors.   3. Rhetoric—
  United States—History—19th century.   4. Afro-American women—
  Intellectual life.   5. Afro-American—History—Sources.
  I. Logan, Shirley Wilson, date.
  PS663.N4W5   1995
  815'.30809287—dc20
  ISBN 0-8093-1874-1   94-11166
  ISBN 0-8093-1875-X pbk.   CIP

The paper used in this publication meets the minimum requirements of
American National Standard for Information Sciences—Permanence of
Paper for Printed Library Materials, ANSI Z39.48-1984. ∞

CONTENTS

ACKNOWLEDGMENTS

I OWE A DEBT OF GRATITUDE TO MANY COLLEAGUES IN THE DEPART-ment of English at the University of Maryland whose help and encouragement nurtured this project, especially Jeanne Fahnestock, Aletha Hendrickson, Michael Marcuse, Mary Helen Washington, Carla Peterson, and Sue Oswald. Jacqueline Jones Royster at Ohio State University was particularly supportive. I express appreciation to Karlyn Kohrs Campbell at the University of Minnesota, who granted permission to include her edition of Sojourner Truth's speech and who also led me to new research on Truth's speaking ability through the work of Suzanne Pullon Fitch. Thomas C. Battle, director of the Moorland-Spingarn Research Center at Howard University, and Patricia Willis, curator of American Literature at the Beinecke Rare Book and Manuscript Library, Yale University, also provided encouragement and support. Students in my nineteenth-century rhetoric courses combed the literature for references to these African-American pioneers of public speaking. Frank Johnson was particularly diligent. My research assistant, Psyche Williams, with support from the University of Maryland's Africa and Africa in the Americas Project, spent hours in the library identifying the numerous allusions in Victoria Matthews's speech "The Value of Race Literature." For their strong nexus of support, I thank my family—my mother, Nelsie T. Johnson; my siblings, Thelma, Melva, John, and Harole; my husband, John Logan; and my children, Enid, Malcolm, and Monica. Above all, I thank God.

INTRODUCTION:
MOUNTING THE PLATFORM

THE NINETEENTH CENTURY IN AFRICAN-AMERICAN EXPERIENCE was filled with turmoil and change. Social exigencies multiplied exponentially as those of African descent first confronted slavery and discrimination, then adjustment to newly acquired physical freedom during Reconstruction, followed by mob violence and the struggle to obtain full citizenship. It is an experience that has been described frequently but not fully. Some muffled voices are those of black women, voices that are gradually being restored to full volume. This anthology is designed to contribute to the restoration by presenting the rhetorical responses of black women who spoke and wrote as preambles to action. As Shockley acknowledges, "To counteract this assault upon black freedom, black women writers fought with pen and voice" (110).

In 1871, a black correspondent of *The Christian Recorder*, organ of the African Methodist Episcopal Church, stressed the importance of black lecturers: "While we need some to diffuse literature in the form of journals and periodicals, we also need those who instruct the masses orally, especially those who cannot read, nor will not subscribe for a paper to be read to them" (qtd. in Foner 6). Frederick Douglass in 1870 exhorted that "press, platform, pulpit should continue to direct their energies to the removal of the hardships and wrongs which continue to be the lot of the colored people of this country" (qtd. in Foner 6). In the forefront of those who chose the platform as the vehicle through which to address these "hardships and wrongs" were black women.

One could easily assemble such a collection as this with texts produced solely during the 1890s. In "Woman's Political Future," a speech delivered at the 1893 World's Congress of Representative Women, Frances Ellen Watkins Harper challenged the women in her audience to exert their influence upon the political life of the nation. Black women of that decade, responding to Harper's challenge, perceived themselves on "the threshold of woman's era" and spoke out on numerous occasions. But such an anthology would ignore the often lonely and solo voices of those women, like Maria Stewart in 1832, who were speaking out even before it was considered acceptable for women to speak publicly. It would also ignore Sojourner Truth's brave rhetorical acts and the early speeches of Harper herself, whose rhetorical career spans the second half of the century. For this reason, the anthology begins with Stewart's lecture delivered at the Franklin Hall and her address delivered before the Afric-American Female Intelligence Society of Boston. These speeches are followed by two versions of Sojourner Truth's 1851 speech delivered at the Akron, Ohio, Woman's Rights Convention, with its haunting question to those assembled, "Ar'n't I a Woman?," as well as her May 9, 1867, speech at the First Annual Meeting of the American Equal Rights Association in New York City. Yet, the outpouring of verbal responses generated by the women of the 1890s cannot be ignored; consequently, most of the speeches included were delivered during that decade.

Perhaps the event providing the most rhetorical opportunities for nineteenth-century black women to address predominantly white audiences was the World's Congress of Representative Women. The Congress, part of the Columbian Exposition, was held from May 15 to May 22, 1893, in Chicago. The exposition's alleged purpose was to display the achievements of the Americas to the rest of the world. The women's exhibit, housed in a building designed by a woman architect, was to illuminate the accomplishments of American women. But as Ida B. Wells points out in her autobiography, *Crusade for Justice*, the "United States government had refused her Negro citizens participation therein" (116). Hallie Quinn Brown of Wilberforce, Ohio, requested of Bertha Palmer, head of the Board of Lady Managers of this Congress, to allow her membership in this policy-making body. She was told that membership was by organization rather than by individual and that Brown represented no organization. Prompted by Palmer's response, Brown went to Washington, D.C., to speak to a group of women at the Fifteenth Street Presbyterian Church, requesting that they select her to represent them on this board. While they did not grant her request, the women did organize themselves into the Colored Woman's League as a result of her talk, and according to Elizabeth Davis, they "stepped across the threshold of the home into the wider arena of organized womanhood" (20).

A few black women were eventually invited to participate in the Congress. Fannie Barrier Williams presented one of the major addresses in a session titled "The Solidarity of Human Interests," during which women from France, Spain, England, Canada, and various countries in South America also spoke. Other black participants who spoke were Anna Julia Cooper, from Washington, D.C., and Frances Jackson Coppin, from Philadelphia, both of whom gave remarks following Williams's speech. Frederick Douglass, who presided over the Haitian exhibit, was also on the platform; after Coppin's remarks, he was prevailed upon to speak. May Wright Sewall, editor of the conference proceedings, notes, "Mr. Douglass was the only man who, after the opening session, spoke in the General Congress" (47). Sarah Early, from Wilberforce, Ohio, spoke on "The Organized Efforts of the Colored Women of the South to Improve Their Condition," and Hallie Quinn Brown followed Early's speech with discussion. Frances Harper, from Philadelphia, spoke during an earlier session titled "The Civil and Political Status of Women." Thus a total of six black women's voices were heard during the Congress. Carby suggests that the participation of these black women was less a recognition of their right to be there than it was part of a "discourse of exoticism that pervaded the fair" (5). The board may have been presenting these women as anomalies to the received and accepted views of blacks at the time. This anthology includes two speeches delivered at the Congress—Harper's "Woman's Political Future" and Fannie Barrier Williams's "Intellectual Progress of the Colored Women of the United States since the Emancipation Proclamation"—because of the Congress's unique rhetorical context.

Anna Julia Haywood Cooper, who also spoke at the Congress, lived to be 105 years old and had a long career as an educator and an intellectual. She advocated in particular for the rights of black women. She also spoke out against the inherent racism of white women's organizations, condemned the practice of taking the advancement of successful individuals as indicative of the advancement of a people as a whole, and argued that only when black women had the power collectively to determine their future would the race be able to move forward. Cooper's 1886 speech included

here, "Womanhood a Vital Element in the Regeneration and Progress of a Race," rehearses the plight of women generally and the
Southern black woman in particular for the benefit of Episcopalian clergymen in Washington, D.C. The "raison d'être" for her
book *A Voice from the South*, published six years later, was to
represent the voice of the Southern black woman.

Any study of the rhetoric of nineteenth-century black women
must also be a study of the black women's club movement. It has
been suggested that the rhetoric of Ida Wells had more to do with
the development of black women's clubs at the beginning of the
1890s than that of any other single person.[1] Wells's speech at the
testimonial in her honor in New York City and the responses
it evoked represented a turning point in such organizations; her
cause became a unifying force. After the testimonial, women such
as Victoria Matthews, Susan McKinney, and Josephine St. Pierre
Ruffin began organizing clubs in New York, Brooklyn, and Boston. When Wells was maligned in the press, all black women felt
the sting. It was in response to an open letter by John W. Jacks,
president of the Missouri Press Association, questioning the morals and integrity of black women, that Josephine St. Pierre Ruffin
sent out a call for women to gather in defense of themselves,
which resulted in the assembling of the First Congress of Colored
Women in 1895. Arguably, then, one can say that Wells's antilynch-
ing rhetoric led to the national organization of black women's
clubs.

Victoria Earle Matthews, the last speaker in this anthology, is
probably the least well known of those presented here, yet she
was quite active in the organizing of the early black women's
clubs, serving as the chair of the executive committee of the Federation of Afro-American Women. Matthews, one of the major
organizers of the testimonial held in Lyric Hall in New York to
honor Ida Wells in 1892, also traveled throughout the South and
exposed the conditions faced by young black women, especially
in the rural districts. Her speech "The Value of Race Literature"
was delivered at the first National Conference of Colored Women
held in Boston in July 1895. One of the primary goals of this
gathering of representatives from various black women's clubs
was, according to Josephine St. Pierre Ruffin, president of the

conference, "to elevate and dignify colored American woman-hood" (E. Davis 19). Matthews appeared on the program with such luminaries as William Lloyd Garrison, T. Thomas Fortune, and Booker T. Washington's wife, Margaret Murray Washington. Matthews's speech addressed the value of literature produced by blacks, arguing for one of the earliest definitions of "race litera-ture" as "all the writings emanating from a distinct class—not necessarily race matter." At the same time, however, she recog-nizes a need for this distinction based on the unique experience of black people in this country. Matthews claims a literature that is and will be different from but not inferior to that produced by others. The debate as to whether black literature should define itself out of the mainstream still rages in contemporary arguments about the need for separate courses in African-American literature within English departments. Matthews anticipates these contem-porary objections in her speech and calls for "thoughtful, well-defined and intelligently placed efforts . . . to serve as counter-ir-ritants" to the prevailing depictions of the race by Anglo-Saxons. A later speech by Matthews, "The Awakening of the Afro-Ameri-can Woman," is also included as an example of her accommoda-tion of material to a sharply different audience.

This anthology contains a total of eleven speeches by seven nineteenth-century women. Some of the speeches were chosen because of their historical significance. Maria Stewart's Franklin Hall speech and Sojourner Truth's speech at the 1851 Woman's Rights Convention in Ohio fall into this category. Others were chosen because they are not readily accessible, like Victoria Mat-thews's "The Value of Race Literature" and "The Awakening of the Afro-American Woman." But they all offer unique rhetorical strategies from women wrestling with unique problems.

A speech is an oral event. Since the text of a speech is not its performance, the printed version can only, at best, approxi-mate what was actually said on each occasion. Maria Stewart's and Anna Cooper's texts are taken from their own editions of speeches and essays. Changes were doubtless made for publica-tion. Ida Wells's speech was taken from a periodical edited by the sponsor of the event, who probably acquired it from Wells. Harper's and Williams's speeches are taken from edited conference proceedings. The texts of Matthews's speeches exist in special collections as unpublished manuscripts of unclear origin. Sojourner Truth's speeches, as included in compiled versions of her *Narrative* and in various articles and histories, were all transcribed by others. Notions about revisions prior to delivery and after publication of these speeches must be essentially speculative, for their authors left no paper trail.

I have limited editorial intervention to identifying notes and bracketed clarifications of sentences, words, or abbreviations, designed to make the speeches more accessible to modern readers. Titles of books, pamphlets, and newspapers have been italicized consistently within a speech. For the most part, original spelling, capitalization, punctuation, and paragraphing have been retained. My goal was to reconstruct the rhetorical context and to let the women speak. What they have to say transcends the constraints of the printed page. Listen.

NOTE

1. For an overview of Wells's contribution to the development of black women's clubs see Giddings, especially chapters 4 and 5.

NINETEENTH-CENTURY AFRICAN-AMERICAN WOMEN: A RHETORICAL TIMELINE

1800–1829	1830–1849	1850–1859	1860–1869
Completion of African Meeting House, Boston (1806)	Garrison published first issue of *The Liberator* (1831)	The Fugitive Slave Law (1850)	Civil War (1861–65)
AME Church organized with Richard Allen in Philadelphia (1816)	Nat Turner's Rebellion (1831)	Sojourner Truth, Speech Delivered to the Woman's Rights Convention (1851)	Emancipation Proclamation (1863)
	Maria W. Stewart, Lecture Delivered at the Franklin Hall (1832)	Mary Ann Shadd Cary, *The Provincial Freeman* (1854)	Frances Ellen Watkins Harper, "We Are All Bound Up Together" speech delivered to the Eleventh Woman's Rights Convention (1866)
	Maria W. Stewart, An Address Delivered Before the Afric-American Female Intelligence Society of Boston (1832)	Frances Ellen Watkins Harper, "The Education and Elevation of the Colored Race" (1854)	
	First black colleges established: Cheyney State, Avery, Lincoln, Wilberforce (1837–1856)	Sarah Parker Remond began her speaking career (1856)	Sojourner Truth, Speech delivered to the American Equal Rights Association (1867)
	Narrative of Frederick Douglass (1845)		Fourteenth Amendment ratified (1868)
	First Woman's Rights Convention, Seneca Falls (1848)		

Continued on the next page

NINETEENTH-CENTURY AFRICAN-AMERICAN WOMEN: A RHETORICAL TIMELINE (*continued*)

1870–1879	1880–1889	1890–1899
Sojourner Truth, Petition for the granting of Western lands to freedmen (1870)	49 blacks reported lynched (1882) 53 lynched (1883)	Frances Ellen Watkins Harper, "Duty to Dependent Races," National Council of Women of the United States, *Transactions* (Philadelphia, 1891)
Fifteenth Amendment ratified (1870)	51 lynched (1884) 74 lynched (1885)	Ida B. Wells, "Southern Horrors" (1892) Ida B. Wells, "Lynch Law in All
Frances Ellen Watkins Harper, "The Great Problem to Be Solved" (1875)	74 lynched (1886) 70 lynched (1887) 69 lynched (1888)	Its Phases" (1893) Anna Julia Haywood Cooper, *A Voice from the South* (1892) The World's Congress of Repre-
Hayes-Tilden Compromise (1877) (end of Reconstruction)	94 lynched (1889)* Anna Julia Haywood Cooper, "Womanhood a Vital Element in the Regeneration and Progress of a Race" (1886)	sentative Women at the Columbian Exposition, Chicago (1893). *Speakers*: Fannie Williams, Frances Harper, Anna Cooper, Frances Coppin, Sarah Early, Hallie Brown Ida B. Wells, *The Reason Why* (1893)
	Henry Grady, "The New South" (1886)	Gertrude Mossell, *The Work of the Afro-American Woman* (1894) Ida B. Wells, *A Red Record* (1895)
	Frances Ellen Watkins Harper, "The Woman's Christian Temperance Union and the Colored Woman" (1888)	Booker T. Washington, Atlanta Exposition Address (1895) Victoria Earle Matthews, "The Value of Race Literature" (1895) National Association of Colored Women and *The Women's Era* (1896) Victoria Earle Matthews, "The Awakening of the Afro-American Woman" (1897)

* Statistics on lynching vary widely with sources; these statistics come from Bennett, 500–504.

WITH PEN AND VOICE

1 MARIA W. STEWART
(1803–1879)

> They would drive us to a strange land. But before I go,
> the bayonet shall pierce me through. African rights and
> liberty is a subject that ought to fire the breast of every
> free man of color in these United States and excite in his
> bosom a lively, deep, decided, and heartfelt interest.
>
> —Maria W. Stewart, "An Address Delivered at the African
> Masonic Hall"

AT THE AGE OF TWENTY-NINE, MARIA W. STEWART BECAME THE
first American woman to speak publicly to a mixed group and to
leave texts of her addresses.[1] This first speech was a "Lecture Delivered at the Franklin Hall" in Boston on September 21, 1832.
Aside from this bold act, the details of Stewart's life are sparse.
She was born in Hartford, Connecticut, in 1803 and was orphaned
at five, after which she went to live with a clergyman's family
until the age of fifteen, where "the seeds of piety and virtue [were]
early sown" in her mind (Stewart 3). Although she received no
formal education, her years "bound out" in the home of the clergyman gave her access to books, possibly including material on
the art of public address, and fostered her desire for knowledge.
Stewart subsequently supported herself as a domestic servant. In
1826, she married James W. Stewart and settled in Boston. Wid-
owed three years later and cheated out of her husband's estate,
she developed a deep commitment to religious and political activ-
ism. In 1831 William Lloyd Garrison and Isaac Knapp, publishers
of the abolitionist newspaper *The Liberator*, printed her first treatise, *Religion and the Pure Principles of Morality, The Sure Foundation on Which We Must Build*. Excerpts from this document appeared in the October 8, 1831, edition of the paper. Of the two
speeches included in this anthology, her first, "An Address Delivered Before the Afric-American Female Intelligence Society of
Boston," appeared in *The Liberator* for April 28, 1832. The second
speech and the first before a mixed group was the "Lecture De-

livered at the Franklin Hall" on September 21, 1832. Because of
its historical significance as the first public lecture by an American
woman, it appears first in the anthology.

Stewart was greatly influenced by the activities of David Walker,
a black abolitionist who had moved to Boston from North Carolina. In 1829 he published a seventy-six page pamphlet, *Appeal,
in Four Articles; Together with a Preamble, to the Coloured Citizens
of the World, but in Particular and Very Expressly, to Those of the
United States of America,* which alarmed abolitionists and slaveholders alike with its strong call for armed resistance against slavery. Stewart mentions him by name in her first published essay,
Religion and the Pure Principles of Morality.[2] Her subsequent
speeches burn with the same fiery rhetoric Walker used in his pro-
vocative pamphlet, an admixture of the religious and the militant.

Early nineteenth-century opposition to women's speaking publicly was strong. What must it have been like for Stewart and
other early women orators? No records exist describing the reac-
tions of Stewart's audiences to her speeches. But she expresses in
her first published essay a sense of isolation: "I stand alone in your
midst, exposed to the fiery darts of the devil, and to the assaults
of wicked men" (Stewart 21). She may have indeed been alone in
her pioneering act as the first American woman to speak before
a mixed group. Yellin speculates that white female abolitionist
readers of Garrison's *Liberator* must have known of her. Yet those
women who later spoke out recognized Angelina Grimké, not
Stewart, as their oratorical ancestor; "either racism or class bias—
or both—prevented them from identifying with Stewart" (Yellin
48). In her "Farewell Address to Her Friends in the City of Boston" of September 21, 1833, Stewart expresses her disappointment
with the poor reception she received. This final address clearly
implicates the people of Boston in a negative campaign against
her year of public speaking. In it, she justifies her behavior by
citing biblical and historical foremothers—judges, queens, mes-
sengers of God, preachers, philosophers, and orators. Inspired by
God, Stewart persisted in the face of opposition from the black
community of Boston. But finally she abandoned her efforts, pro-
claiming, "I am about to leave you, perhaps, never more to return.

For I find it is no use for me as an individual to try to make myself useful among my color in this city. It was contempt for my moral and religious opinions in private that drove me thus before a public" (78). Her public speaking career lasted exactly one year— from September 21, 1832, to September 21, 1833. During this time she delivered four addresses in Boston: the two included here, "An Address Delivered at the African Masonic Hall" on February 27, 1833, and the farewell address. Campbell has suggested that the challenge Stewart faced "illustrates the inevitable link between any rhetorical effort and the struggle for woman's rights" (*Critical Study* 19). Women needed to gain the right to speak before they would be allowed to address other issues.[3]

Soon after delivering her farewell address, she moved to New York, continued her education, and was active in black literary societies for women. She became a public school teacher and in 1852 migrated to Baltimore and finally to Washington, D.C., in 1863. After the Civil War, Stewart joined Washington's public school system and later became matron of Freedmen's Hospital. In 1879, the last year of her life, she reprinted the speeches and writings of *Productions of Mrs. Maria Stewart, Presented to the First African Baptist Church and Society, in the City of Boston*, published in Boston in 1835, under the title *Meditations from the Pen of Mrs. Maria W. Stewart*, adding new introductory material.

It comes as no surprise that an intensely religious woman speaking publicly in 1832 would seek support and justification in the Scriptures. In keeping with her direct manner, the "Lecture Delivered at the Franklin Hall" opens with a question, immediately drawing her black audience into her deliberations.[4] Aware that by speaking publicly she is outside a "woman's sphere" (O'Connor 24), she defines her act as a response to "spiritual interrogation" from God. Stewart understood that slavery of the body was not nearly as devastating as slavery of the soul and directs her charges not so much against the plight of the Southern enslaved as against the abuses experienced by Northern free people of color. In particular, this speech attacks discriminatory hiring practices that prevented young black women from acquiring jobs other than those related to domestic service, a service that she does recognize as having value. She challenges her people to self-improvement in the face of these difficulties. Like David Walker in his *Appeal*, Stewart addresses her concerns specifically to blacks, but at several points in the Franklin Hall speech, she takes a rhetorical turn and confronts the white members—male and female—of her audience.

The second speech included here, "An Address Delivered Before the Afric-American Female Intelligence Society of Boston," was published in *The Liberator* on April 28, 1832, and we can assume that it was delivered close to this date. While the Franklin Hall speech was the first to a mixed group, Stewart's address to this society, established in 1831 for the purpose of promoting education and morality among the black women of Massachusetts, was her first public lecture. The opening of this speech indicates her keen awareness that she would face objections, but she declares her intention to prevail because she has been inspired by God. As O'Connor points out, "Any woman who had the temerity to step forth upon the public platform to address a promiscuous assembly was considered by most people in nineteenth-century America to be without two of these characteristics [high moral character and goodwill]" (134). For this reason, many early women speakers opened their texts with the claim that they had been called to speak out, compelled by a religious power to do "God's work." As Stewart says in this address, "I believe that God has fired my soul with a holy zeal for his cause." Fully one-third of this speech invokes the biblical day of retribution and reiterates Stewart's claim to a God-inspired calling to come forward. In the remaining portion, she admonishes the women to treat each other more kindly and appeals to historical precedent for examples of other groups who have united for self-improvement. In closing, she bids the women to exert their special influence as women, a theme that prefigures Anna Julia Cooper's 1886 speech to the Convocation of Colored Clergy, in which she too exhorts women to use their "feminine" attributes to advance the race.

Taken together, these two speeches reveal the thinking of a biblically inspired woman, keenly aware of her rhetorical constraints, who was compelled by God and the plight of her people to advocate for social action.

NOTES

1. See O'Connor for a discussion of British-born Frances Wright who "shocked American sensibilities" (Sterling 154n) when on July 4, 1828, she delivered her first public speech.

2. For a careful reconstruction of Stewart's Boston years and of David Walker's influence, see Richardson (3–27), who suggests that Walker may have used the position of James Stewart, a ship's outfitter or shipping master, to help him disseminate his pamphlets.

3. See Campbell (*Critical Study* 17–36) for discussion of Stewart's efforts in the larger context of early feminist abolitionist rhetoric. She explores the extent to which the prohibitions against women speaking constrained pioneer rhetors like Stewart, Truth, and the Grimké sisters.

4. See Richardson (45–49) and Campbell (*Key Texts* 3–10) for documentation of scriptural sources for much of Stewart's language in the Franklin Hall speech. For example, the syntactic pattern of the opening paragraph of the speech echoes 2 Kings 7:3, 4: "Why sit we here until we die? If we say, We will enter into the city, then the famine is in the city, and we shall die there: and if we sit still here, we die also. Now therefore come, and let us fall unto the host of the Syrians: if they save us alive, we shall live; and if they kill us, we shall but die." Stewart herself acknowledges this borrowing, which was a common practice among early women rhetors. Knowledge of the Bible enhanced the ethos of these pioneer speakers.

LECTURE DELIVERED AT THE FRANKLIN HALL
(1832)

Why sit ye here and die? if we say we will go to a foreign land, the famine and the pestilence are there, and there we shall die. If we sit here, we shall die. Come let us plead our cause before the whites: if they save us alive, we shall live—and if they kill us, we shall but die.

Methinks I heard a spiritual interrogation—"Who shall go forward, and take off the reproach that is cast upon the people of color? Shall it be a woman?" And my heart made this reply—"If it is thy will, be it even so, Lord Jesus!"

I have heard much respecting the horrors of slavery; but may Heaven forbid that the generality of my color throughout these United States should experience any more of its horrors than to be a servant of servants, or hewers of wood and drawers of water! Tell us no more of southern slavery; for with few exceptions, although I may be very erroneous in my opinion, yet I consider our condition but little better than that. Yet, after all, methinks there are no chains so galling as the chains of ignorance—no fetters so binding as those that bind the soul, and exclude it from the vast field of useful and scientific knowledge. O, had I received the advantages of an early education, my ideas would, ere now, have expanded far and wide; but, alas! I possess nothing but moral capability—no teachings but the teachings of the Holy Spirit.

I have asked several individuals of my sex, who transact business for themselves, if providing our girls were to give them the most satisfactory references, they would not be willing to grant them an equal opportunity with others? Their reply has been—for their own part, they had no objection; but as it was not the custom, were they to take them into their employ, they would be in danger of losing the public patronage.

And such is the powerful force of prejudice. Let our girls possess whatever amiable qualities of soul they may; let their characters be fair and spotless as innocence itself; let their natural taste and ingenuity be what they may; it is impossible for scarce an

6

individual of them to rise above the condition of servants. Ah! why is this cruel and unfeeling distinction? Is it merely because God has made our complexion to vary? If it be, O shame to soft, relenting humanity! "Tell it not in Gath! publish it not in the streets of Askelon!" Yet, after all, methinks were the American free people of color to turn their attention more assiduously to moral worth and intellectual improvement, this would be the result: prejudice would gradually diminish, and the whites would be compelled to say, unloose those fetters!

Though black their skins as shades of night
Their hearts are pure, their souls are white.

Few white persons of either sex, who are calculated for anything else, are willing to spend their lives and bury their talents in performing mean, servile labor. And such is the horrible idea that I entertain respecting a life of servitude, that if I conceived of there being no possibility of my rising above the condition of servant, I would gladly hail death as a welcome messenger. O, horrible idea, indeed! to possess noble souls aspiring after high and honorable acquirements, yet confined by the chains of ignorance and poverty to lives of continual drudgery and toil. Neither do I know of any who have enriched themselves by spending their lives as house domestics, washing windows, shaking carpets, brushing boots, or tending upon gentlemen's tables. I can but die for expressing my sentiments: and I am as willing to die by the sword as the pestilence; for I am a true born American; your blood flows in my veins, and your spirit fires my breast.

I observed a piece in the *Liberator* a few months since, stating that the colonizationists had published a work respecting us, asserting that we were lazy and idle. I confute them on that point. Take us generally as a people, we are neither lazy nor idle; and considering how little we have to excite or stimulate us, I am almost astonished that there are so many industrious and ambitious ones to be found; although I acknowledge, with extreme sorrow, that there are some who never were and never will be serviceable to society. And have you not a similar class among yourselves?

Again. It was asserted that we were "a ragged set, crying for

liberty." I reply to it, the whites have so long and so loudly proclaimed the theme of equal rights and privileges, that our souls
have caught the flame also, ragged as we are. As far as our merit
deserves, we feel a common desire to rise above the condition of
servants and drudges. I have learnt, by bitter experience, that continual hard labor deadens the energies of the soul, and benumbs
the faculties of the mind; ideas become confined, the mind barren,
and, like the scorching sands of Arabia, produces nothing; or like
the uncultivated brings forth thorns and thistles.

Again, continual and hard labor irritates our tempers and sours
our dispositions; the whole system becomes worn out with toil
and fatigue; nature herself becomes almost exhausted, and we care
little whether we live or die. It is true, that the free people of color
throughout these United States are neither bought nor sold, nor
under the lash of the cruel driver; many obtain a comfortable support; but few, if any, have an opportunity of becoming rich and
independent; and the enjoyments we most pursue are as unprofit-
able to us as the spider's web or the floating bubbles that vanish
into air. As servants, we are respected; but let us presume to aspire
higher, our employer regards us no longer. And were it not that
the King eternal has declared that Ethiopia shall stretch forth her
hands unto God, I should indeed despair.

I do not consider it derogatory, my friends, for persons to live
out to service. There are many whose inclination leads them to
aspire no higher; and I would highly commend the performance
of almost anything for an honest livelihood; but where constitu-
tional strength is wanting, labor of this kind, in its mildest form,
is painful. And doubtless many are the prayers that have ascended
to Heaven from Afric's daughters for strength to perform their
work. Oh, many are the tears that have been shed for the want
of that strength! Most of our color have dragged out a miserable
existence of servitude from the cradle to the grave. And what
literary acquirement can be made, or useful knowledge derived,
from either maps, books, or charts, by those who continually
drudge from Monday morning until Sunday noon? O, ye fairer
sisters, whose hands are never soiled, whose nerves and muscles
are never strained, go learn by experience! Had we had the opportunity that you have had to improve our moral and mental

faculties, what would have hindered our intellects from being as
bright, and our manners from being as dignified as yours? Had
it been our lot to have been nursed in the lap of affluence and
ease, and to have basked beneath the smiles and sunshine of fortune, should we not have naturally supposed that we were never
made to toil? And why are not our forms as delicate, and our
constitutions as slender, as yours? Is not the workmanship as curious and complete? Have pity upon us, have pity upon us, O ye
who have hearts to feel for other's woes; for the hand of God has
touched us. Owing to the disadvantages under which we labor,
there are many flowers among us that are

   . . . born to bloom unseen
And waste their fragrance on the desert air.

My beloved brethren, as Christ has died in vain for those who
will not accept his offered mercy, so will it be vain for the advocates of freedom to spend their breath in our behalf, unless with
united hearts and souls you make some mighty efforts to raise
your sons and daughters from the horrible state of servitude and
degradation in which they are placed. It is upon you that woman
depends; she can do but little besides using her influence; and it
is for her sake and yours that I have come forward and made myself a hissing and a reproach among the people; for I am also one
of the wretched and miserable daughters of the descendants of
fallen Africa. Do you ask, why are you wretched and miserable?
I reply, look at many of the most worthy and most interesting of
us doomed to spend our lives in gentlemen's kitchens. Look at
our young men, smart, active and energetic, with souls filled with
ambitious fire; if they look forward, alas! What are their prospects? They can be nothing but the humblest laborers, on account
of their dark complexions; hence many of them lose their ambition, and become worthless. Look at our middle-aged men, clad
in their rusty plaids and coats; in winter, every cent they earn
goes to buy their wood and pay their rents; the poor wives also
toil beyond their strength, to help support their families. Look at
our aged sires, whose heads are whitened with the frosts of seventy winters, with their old wood-saws on their backs. Alas, what

keeps us so? Prejudice, ignorance and poverty. But ah! methinks our oppression is soon to come to an end; yea, before the Majesty of heaven, our groans and cries have reached the ears of the Lord of Sabaoth. As the prayers and tears of Christians will avail the finally impenitent nothing; neither will the prayers and tears of the friends of humanity avail us anything, unless we possess a spirit of virtuous emulation within our breasts. Did the pilgrims, when they first landed on these shores, quietly compose themselves and say, "The Britons have all the money and all the power, and we must continue their servants forever?" Did they sluggishly sigh and say, "Our lot is hard, the Indians own the soil, and we cannot cultivate it?" No; they first made powerful efforts to raise themselves, and then God raised up those illustrious patriots, WASHINGTON and LAFAYETTE, to assist and defend them. And, my brethren, have you made a powerful effort? Have you prayed the legislature for mercy's sake to grant you all the rights and privileges of free citizens, that your daughters may rise to that degree of respectability which true merit deserves, and your sons above the servile situations which most of them fill?

AN ADDRESS DELIVERED BEFORE THE AFRIC-AMERICAN FEMALE INTELLIGENCE SOCIETY OF BOSTON
(1832)

THE FROWNS OF THE WORLD SHALL NEVER DISCOURAGE ME, NOR ITS smiles flatter me; for with the help of God, I am resolved to withstand the fiery darts of the devil, and the assaults of wicked men. The righteous are as bold as a lion, but the wicked fleeth when no man pursueth. I fear neither men nor devils; for the God in whom I trust is able to deliver me from the rage and malice of my enemies, and from them that rise up against me. The only motive that has prompted me to raise my voice in your behalf, my friends, is because I have discovered that religion is held in low repute among some of us; and purely to promote the cause of Christ, and the good of souls, in the hope that others more experienced, more able and talented than myself, might go forward and do likewise. I expect to render a strict, a solemn, and an awful account to God for the motives that have prompted me to exertion, and for those with which I shall address you this evening.

What I have to say concerns the whole of us as Christians and as a people; and if you will be so kind as to give me a hearing this once, you shall receive the incense of a grateful heart.

The day is coming, my friends, and I rejoice in that day, when the secrets of all hearts shall be manifested before saints and angels, men and devils. It will be a great day of joy and rejoicing to the humble followers of Christ, but a day of terror and dismay to hypocrites and unbelievers. Of that day and hour knoweth no man, no, not even the angels in heaven, but the Father only. The dead that are in Christ shall be raised first. Blessed is he that shall have a part in the first resurrection. Ah, methinks I hear the finally impenitent crying, "Rocks and mountains! fall upon us, and hide us from the wrath of the Lamb, and from him that sitteth upon the throne!"

High on a cloud our God shall come,
Bright thrones prepare his way;

Thunder and darkness, fire and storm,
Lead on the dreadful day.

Christ shall descend in the clouds of heaven, surrounded by
ten thousand of his saints and angels, and it shall be very tempestuous round about him; and before him shall be gathered all nations, and kindred, and tongues, and people; and every knee shall
bow, and every tongue confess; they also that pierced him shall
look upon him, and mourn. Then shall the King separate the righteous from the wicked, as a shepherd divideth the sheep from the
goats, and shall place the righteous on his right hand, and the
wicked upon his left. Then, says Christ, shall be weeping, and
wailing, and gnashing of teeth, when ye shall see Abraham and
the prophets, sitting in the kingdom of heaven, and ye yourselves
thrust out. Then shall the righteous shine forth in the kingdom
of their Father as the sun. He that hath ears to hear, let him hear.
The poor despised followers of Christ will not then regret their
sufferings here; they shall be carried by angels into Abraham's
bosom, and shall be comforted; and the Lord God shall wipe away
their tears. You will then be convinced before assembled multi-
tudes, whether they strove to promote the cause of Christ, or
whether they sought for gain or applause. "Strive to enter in at
the strait gate; for many, I say unto you, shall seek to enter in,
and shall not be able. For except your righteousness shall exceed
the righteousness of the Scribes and Pharisees, ye shall in no wise
enter into the kingdom of heaven."

Ah, methinks I see this people lying in wickedness; and as the
Lord liveth, and as your souls live, were it not for the few righteous that are to be found among us, we should become as Sodom,
and like unto Gomorrah. Christians have too long slumbered and
slept; sinners stumbled into hell, and still are stumbling, for the
want of Christian exertion; and the devil is going about like a
roaring lion, seeking whom he may devour. And I make bold to
say, that many who profess the name of Christ at the present day,
live so widely different from what becometh the Gospel of our
Lord Jesus Christ, that they cannot and they dare not reason to
the world upon righteousness and judgment to come.

Be not offended because I tell you the truth; for I believe that

God has fired my soul with a holy zeal for his cause. It was God alone who inspired my heart to publish the meditations thereof; and it was done with pure motives of love to your souls, in the hope that Christians might examine themselves, and sinners become pricked in their hearts. It is the word of God, though men and devils may oppose it. It is the word of God; and little did I think that any of the professed followers of Christ would have frowned upon me, and discouraged and hindered its progress.

Ah, my friends, I am speaking as one who expects to give account at the bar of God; I am speaking as a dying mortal to dying mortals. I fear there are many who have named the name of Jesus at the present day, that strain at a gnat and swallow a camel; they neither enter into the kingdom of heaven themselves, nor suffer others to enter in. They would pull the motes out of their brother's eye, when they have a beam in their own eye. And were our blessed Lord and Saviour, Jesus Christ, upon the earth, I believe he would say of many that are called by his name, "O, ye hypocrites, ye generation of vipers, how can you escape the damnation of hell." I have enlisted in the holy warfare, and Jesus is my captain; and the Lord's battle I mean to fight, until my voice expire in death. I expect to be hated of all men, and persecuted even unto death, for righteousness and the truth's sake.

A few remarks upon moral subjects and I close. I am a strong advocate for the cause of God, and for the cause of freedom. I am not your enemy, but a friend both to you and to your children. Suffer me, then, to express my sentiments but this once, however severe they may appear to be, and then hereafter let me sink into oblivion, and let my name die in forgetfulness.

Had the ministers of the gospel shunned the very appearance of evil; had they faithfully discharged their duty, whether we would have heard them or not; we should have been a very different people from what we now are; but they have kept the truth as it were, hid from our eyes, and have cried, "Peace, Peace!" when there was no peace; they have plastered us with untempered mortar, and have been as it were blind leaders of the blind.

It appears to me that there are no people under the heavens, so unkind and so unfeeling towards their own, as are the descendants of fallen Africa. I have been something of a traveller in my day;

and the general cry among the people is, "Our own color are our greatest opposers"; and even the whites say that we are greater enemies towards each other, than they are towards us. Shall we be a hissing and a reproach among the nations of the earth any longer! Shall they laugh us to scorn forever? We might become a highly respectable people; respectable we now consider ourselves, but we might become a highly distinguished and intelligent people. And how? In convincing the world, by our own efforts, however feeble, that nothing is wanting on our part but opportunity. Without these efforts, we shall never be a people, nor our descendants after us.

But God has said, that Ethiopia shall stretch forth her hands unto him. True, but God uses means to bring about his purposes; and unless the rising generation manifest a different temper and disposition towards each other from what we have manifested, the generation following will never be an enlightened people. We this day are considered as one of the most degraded races upon the face of the earth. It is useless for us any longer to sit with our hands folded, reproaching the whites; for that will never elevate us. All the nations of the earth have distinguished themselves, and have shown forth a noble and a gallant spirit. Look at the suffering Greeks! Their proud souls revolted at the idea of serving a tyrannical nation, who were no better than themselves, and perhaps not so good. They made a mighty effort and arose; their souls were knit together in the holy bonds of love and union; they were united, and came off victorious. Look at the French in the late revolution! no traitors among them, to expose their plans to the crowned heads of Europe! "Liberty or Death!" was their cry. And the Haytians [sic], though they have not been acknowledged as a nation, yet their firmness of character, and independence of spirit have been greatly admired, and high applauded. Look at the Poles, a feeble people! They rose against three hundred thousand mighty men of Russia; and though they did not gain the conquest, yet they obtained the name of gallant Poles. And even the wild Indians of the forest are more united than ourselves. Insult one of them, and you insult a thousand. They also have contended for their rights and privileges, and are held in higher repute than we are.

And why is it, my friends, that we are despised above all the nations upon the earth? Is it merely because our skins are tinged with a sable hue? No, nor will I ever believe that it is. What then is it; Oh, it is because that we and our fathers have dealt treacherously one with another, and because many of us now possess that envious and malicious disposition, that we had rather die than see each other rise an inch above a beggar. No gentle methods are used to promote love and friendship among us, but much is done to destroy it. Shall we be a hissing and a reproach among the nations of the earth any longer? Shall they laugh us to scorn forever?

Ingratitude is one of the worst passions that reigns in the human breast; it is this that cuts the tender fibres of the soul; for it is impossible for us to love those who are ungrateful towards us. "Behold," says that wise man, Soloman [sic], counting one by one, "a man have I found in a thousand, but a woman among all those have I not found."

I have sometimes thought, that God had almost departed from among us. And why? Because Christ has said, if we say we love the Father, and hate our brother, we are liars, and the truth is not in us; and certainly if we were the true followers of Christ, I think we could not show such a disposition towards each other as we do: for God is all love.

A lady of high distinction among us, observed to me, that I might never expect your homage. God forbid! I ask it not. But I beseech you to deal with gentleness and godly sincerity towards me; and there is not one of you, my dear friends, who has given me a cup of cold water in the name of the Lord, or soothed the sorrows of my wounded heart, but God will bless, not only you, but your children for it. Cruel indeed, are those that indulge such an opinion respecting me as that.

Finally, I have exerted myself both for your temporal and eternal welfare, as far as I am able; and my soul has been so discouraged within me, that I have almost been induced to exclaim, "Would to God that my tongue hereafter might cleave to the roof of my mouth, and become silent forever!" and then I have felt that the Christian has no time to be idle, and I must be active, knowing that the night of death cometh, in which no man can work; and my mind has become raised to such an extent, that I will willingly die for the cause that I have espoused; for I cannot die in a more glorious cause than in the defence of God and his laws.

O woman, woman! upon you I call; for upon your exertions almost entirely depends whether the rising generation shall be any thing more than we have been or not. O woman, woman! your example is powerful, your influence great; it extends over your husbands and over your children, and throughout the circle of your acquaintance. Then let me exhort you to cultivate among yourselves a spirit of Christian love and unity, having charity one for another, without which all our goodness is as sounding brass, and as a tinkling cymbal. And O, my God, I beseech thee to grant that the nations of the earth may hiss at us no longer! O suffer them not to laugh us to scorn forever!

2 SOJOURNER TRUTH
(c. 1797–1883)

> My name was Isabella; but when I left the house of
> bondage, I left everything behind. I wa'n't goin' to keep
> nothin' of Egypt on me, an' so I went to the Lord an'
> asked him to give me a new name. And the Lord gave me
> Sojourner, because I was to travel up an' down the land,
> showin' the people their sins, an' bein' a sign unto them.
> Afterward I told the Lord I wanted another name, 'cause
> everybody else had two names; and the Lord gave me
> Truth, because I was to declare the truth to the people.
>
> —Sojourner Truth as rendered by Harriet Beecher Stowe in
> "Sojourner Truth, the Libyan Sibyl"

THE MAJOR CONSTRAINT ASSOCIATED WITH ANY ATTEMPT TO
assess the life and works of Sojourner Truth is that one is entirely
dependent upon secondary sources. Nothing written by Truth
herself, in her own hand, is available. Only snatches of remembrances, newspaper accounts, anecdotes, transcriptions, and impressionistic sketches remain as evidence that she lived and spoke.
This state of affairs is a consequence of Truth's never learning to
read or write. Historians have speculated as to why she remained
illiterate, especially in the state of New York where it was not
against the law to teach slaves to read and where, in 1810, slaveholding citizens of the state were required by law to teach their
slaves to read the Bible in preparation for emancipation.[1] While
questions surrounding Truth's literacy may be important for biographers to answer, they become rhetorically significant only to
the extent that they help to authenticate her speech texts. In spite
of the imperfections, were it not for the efforts of others to record
the actions and words of this pioneer rhetor, we would have no
texts at all. I will return to the issue of appropriated texts in the
consideration of Truth's Akron speech.

Sojourner Truth was born in New York State around 1797; the
exact date is not known.[2] Named Isabella, she was sold away from

her parents at the age of nine years and was subsequently sold to
a series of other owners. According to one source, she was married in 1815 and had five children, one boy and four girls (Lowe
181). She escaped from slavery in 1827 and lived with a Quaker
family until 1828, when, according to state law, all slaves were to
be emancipated. She moved to New York City, became a domestic worker, and joined a religious commune. In 1843, at that time
about forty-six years old, Isabella declared herself to be Sojourner
Truth, called by God to travel and preach. In this manner she
began her career as a lecturer. She told her story across Long Island
and entered Connecticut and then Massachusetts, where she joined
the Northampton Association of Education and Industry. While
in Massachusetts, she met some of the leading abolitionists, including William Lloyd Garrison, Frederick Douglass, David Ruggles, Parker Pillsbury, and Wendell Phillips (Bernard 138–144).
During her affiliation with the association, she "honed her speaking skills . . . entrancing well-educated audiences with her vision-
ary observations" (Patten 3). In 1850, with the help of Olive Gilbert, a friend from the Northampton Association, the *Narrative
of Sojourner Truth* was published. Truth sold her story to antislavery and women's rights gatherings.

   In May of 1851, Truth attended the second Woman's Rights
Convention in Akron, Ohio. The first in Ohio had been held a
year earlier in Salem, and membership had increased considerably
by the time of this second gathering. The only black woman in
attendance (A. Davis 61), Truth was a spectator on the first day,
peddling her book at intermission. On the second day, during a
particularly stormy session, ministers from several denominations
spoke out against many of the fifteen proposed resolutions on such
topics as common-law marriages, labor conditions, and education. Many of the women there did not want Truth to speak for
fear that their cause would be damaged by association with the
slavery issue. They implored, "Don't let her speak, Mrs. Gage, it
will ruin us. Every newspaper in the land will have our cause
mixed up with abolition and niggers, and we shall be utterly denounced" (Truth 132). Frances D. Gage, who presided at the convention, described Truth's appearance and the crowd's reaction to
her commanding presence as she approached the pulpit to speak:

Slowly from her seat in the corner rose Sojourner Truth, who, till now, had scarcely lifted her head. "Don't let her speak!" gasped half a dozen in my ear. She moved slowly and solemnly to the front, laid her old bonnet at her feet, and turned her great, speaking eyes to me. There was a hissing sound of disapprobation above and below. I rose and announced "Sojourner Truth," and begged the audience to keep silence for a few moments. The tumult subsided at once, and every eye was fixed on this almost Amazon form, which stood nearly six feet high, head erect, and eye piercing the upper air, like one in a dream. At her first word, there was a profound hush. She spoke in deep tones, which, though not loud, reached every ear in the house, and away through the throng at the doors and windows. (Truth 133)

In spite of Truth's demeanor of disinterest, "crouched against the wall on the corner of the pulpit stair" listening half heartedly, it became apparent as she developed her remarks that she had been listening very carefully to the arguments being put forth. Her speech systematically refutes the previous speakers' claims. First, she rebuts the notion that women are weak and powerless, using her own body and her own experience as counterevidence. Then she calls into question the contention that rights should be distributed on the basis of intellectual acumen. Finally, she rejects one clergyman's biblical argument against rights for women by pointing to the parentage of Christ—God and a woman.

This 1851 speech, best known for its refrain, "Ar'n't /Aren't / Ain't I a Woman?," implies, as historian Giddings observes, that "Black women had already proved their inherent strengths—both physical and psychological. They had undergone a baptism of fire and emerged intact. Therefore, their convictions concerning the rights of women were deeply rooted in experience as well as theory" (55). Interestingly, the speech received little attention at the time it was delivered. As Painter points out, no mention is made of her or her address in the official proceedings of the 1851 CONVENTION (7). Painter also confirms that the speech first appeared, as recorded by Frances Gage, in the 1870s, over twenty years after the event, and was published in Frances Titus's 1878 edition of Truth's *Narrative* (15 n. 9). It grew in popularity after that date.

I have included here two versions of it to highlight the difficulty in working with a speaker such as Truth. One problem with re-producing her speech in writing is the representational idiolect. How did Frances Gage "hear" Truth? One frequently sees it re-ferred to as the "*Ain't* [emphasis mine] I a Woman?" speech, yet in the Gage version the word appears as "*Ar'n't.*" Feminist scholar Haraway offers an explanation for this most commonly antholo-gized rendering:

> That written text represents Truth's speech in the white abolitionist's imagined idiolect of The Slave, the suppos-edly archetypical black plantation slave of the South. The transcription does not provide a southern Afro-American English that any linguist, much less actual speaker, would claim. But it *is* the falsely specific, imagined language that represented the "universal" language of slaves to the liter-ate abolitionist public, and this is the language that has come down to us as Sojourner Truth's "authentic" words. This counterfeit language, undifferentiated into the many Englishes spoken in the New World, reminds us of a hos-tile notion of difference, one that sneaks the masterful un-marked categories in through the back door in the *guise* of the specific, which is made to be not disruptive or deconstructive, but typical. (97)

Campbell's editing, published over 125 years later, removes all dialectical indicators and ungrammatical constructions. Certainly the "authenticity" of such a version could also be questioned. One researcher has uncovered a fragment of an article in the *Kalamazoo* (Michigan) *Telegraph* in which a reporter relates Truth's concern about the way in which her speech is often distorted in print: "People who report her often exaggerate her expressions, put-ting into her mouth the most marked southern dialect, which Sojourner feels is rather taking an unfair advantage of her" (1).[3] Haraway suggests that transcriptions printed in " 'standard' late-twentieth-century American English" may seem "less racist, more 'normal' to hearers who want to forget the diasporas that populated the New World, while making one of its figures into a 'typical' hero" (97). Reflecting on his initial impression of Truth, Douglass seemed particularly annoyed with her manner of speaking:

> I met here [Northampton, Massachusetts] for the first time that strange compound of wit and wisdom, of wild enthusiasm and flint-like common sense, who seemed to feel it her duty to trip me up in my speeches and to ridicule my efforts to speak and act like a person of cultivation and refinement. I allude to Sojourner Truth. She was the genuine specimen of the uncultured negro. She cared very little for elegance of speech or refinement of manners. She seemed to please herself and others best when she put her ideas in the oddest forms.[4] (Terry 442)

This impression suggests that Truth may have been more in control of the ways in which her speech was represented than at first presumed. She may have engaged in a linguistic dissembling for her own reasons. In the case of Truth, since textual authenticity is virtually impossible to achieve, examining various representations seems a reasonable compromise and one that alerts readers to the transcriptive problems and possibilities. In the final analysis, what makes Truth's speech important, after all, are the forceful and compelling arguments she offers in rebuttal to the objections of the ministers, arguments that were clearly effective, however they were vocalized.

After she spoke at the 1851 convention, Truth became a frequent lecturer at various woman's rights gatherings. The second speech included here was delivered at the 1867 American Equal Rights Association (AERA) convention at the Church of the Puritans in New York City. The AERA had been established the previous year at the Eleventh National Woman's Rights Convention with the idea of working for suffrage for black men and all women. Truth, along with other prominent activists, including Elizabeth Cady Stanton, Frances Gage, Charles Remond, and Frederick Douglass, had been invited to speak (Stanton, Anthony, and Gage 182–

183n). However, hostility did develop at this meeting when it became apparent that sympathy centered on support for the Fifteenth
Amendment, which would permit only black men to vote. Davis
explains the controversy in her summary of events: "The major
issue at this convention was the impending enfranchisement of
Black men—and whether the advocates of women's rights were
willing to support Black suffrage even if women were unable to
achieve the vote simultaneously. Elizabeth Cady Stanton and others who believed that because, in their eyes, emancipation had
rendered Black people 'equal' to white women, the vote would
render Black men superior, were absolutely opposed to Black male
suffrage" (A. Davis 72–73).

Truth, unlike Frances Harper and Frederick Douglass, supported
the position that black men should not receive the vote before
women, claiming, "If colored men get their rights, and not colored women get theirs, there will be a bad time about it." At the
1869 AERA convention, which resulted in its split, Harper argued
that "when it was a question of race, she let the lesser question
of sex go. . . . If the nation could only handle one question, she
would not have the black woman put a single straw in the way,
if only the men of the race could obtain what they wanted" (Stanton, Anthony, and Gage 391–392).

Davis suggests that by 1869 Truth had changed her position
and places her on the side of Douglass and Harper (A. Davis 83).
What is clear is that in 1867, based on the text of her speech to
the AERA, Truth sided with the white women who strongly opposed the ratification of the Fifteenth Amendment.

I include here the text as printed in Stanton, Anthony, and Gage's
History of Woman Suffrage, published in 1881. The June 1, 1867,
edition of the *National Anti-Slavery Standard* also contains a slightly
shorter transcription, but the texts are essentially the same. Notice
also a different representation of Truth's language in this 1867 address from the representation by Gage in the 1851 speech.

NOTES

1. See Mabee's article for a causal analysis of Truth's failure to
achieve literacy. He posits a learning disability as the dominant contributing factor and suggests that many of the quotes in which she minimizes

the importance of an education may have been offered as a defense mechanism. However, Mabee fails to consider the impact of gender on Truth, comparing her illiteracy to the success of Frederick Douglass and James W. C. Pennington, both male ex-slaves, in learning to read and write.

2. All biographical material comes from Truth's *Narrative*, unless otherwise indicated.

3. I am indebted to Professor Campbell for this quote, included in personal communication, which comes from a chapter on Truth by Suzanne Pullon Fitch in *Women Public Speakers in the United States, 1800–1925: A Bio-Critical Sourcebook*, ed. Karlyn Kohrs Campbell (Westport, CT: Greenwood Press, 1993).

4. This quote comes from a memoir Douglass wrote around 1894, "What I Found at the Northampton Association," which was included in Sheffeld's *History of Florence* [Massachusetts], 1894, and was reprinted in Terry's article.

SPEECH DELIVERED TO THE WOMAN'S RIGHTS CONVENTION, AKRON, OHIO (1851)

[GAGE VERSION]

"WELL, CHILERN, WHAR DAR IS SO MUCH RACKET DAR MUST BE something out o' kilter. I tink dat 'twixt de niggers of de Souf and de women at de Norf all a talkin' 'bout rights, de white men will be in a fix pretty soon. But what's all dis here talkin' 'bout? Dat man ober dar say dat women needs to be helped into carriages, and lifted ober ditches, and to have de best place every whar. Nobody eber help me into carriages, or ober mud puddles, or gives me any best place [and raising herself to her full hight [*sic*] and her voice to a pitch like rolling thunder, she asked], and ar'n't I a woman? Look at me! Look at my arm! [And she bared her right arm to the shoulder, showing her tremendous muscular power.] I have plowed, and planted, and gathered into barns, and no man could head me—and ar'n't I a woman? I could work as much and eat as much as a man (when I could get it), and bear de lash as well—and ar'n't I a woman? I have borne thirteen chilern and seen 'em mos' all sold off into slavery, and when I cried out with a mother's grief, none but Jesus heard—and ar'n't I a woman? Den dey talks 'bout dis ting in de head—what dis dey call it?" "Intellect," whispered some one near. "Dat's it honey. What's dat got to do with women's rights or niggers' rights? If my cup won't hold but a pint and yourn holds a quart, would n't ye be mean not to let me have my little half-measure full?" And she pointed her significant finger and sent a keen glance at the minister who had made the argument. The cheering was long and loud.

"Den dat little man in black dar, he say women can't have as much rights as man, cause Christ want a woman. Whar did your Christ come from?" Rolling thunder could not have stilled that crowd as did those deep, wonderful tones, as she stood there with outstretched arms and eye of fire. Raising her voice still louder, she repeated, "Whar did your Christ come from? From God and a woman. Man had nothing to do with him." Oh! what a rebuke she gave the little man.

Turning again to another objector, she took up the defense of mother Eve. I cannot follow her through it all. It was pointed, and witty, and solemn, eliciting at almost every sentence deafening applause; and she ended by asserting that "if de fust woman God ever made was strong enough to turn the world upside down, all 'lone, dese togedder [and she glanced her eye over us] ought to be able to turn it back and get it right side up again, and now dey is asking to do it, de men better let em." Long, continued cheering. " 'Bleeged to yo for hearin' on me, and now ole Sojourner ha'n't got nothing more to say."

SPEECH DELIVERED TO THE WOMAN'S RIGHTS CONVENTION, AKRON, OHIO (1851)
[CAMPBELL VERSION]

Well, children, where there is so much racket there must be something out o' kilter. I think that 'twixt the Negroes of the South and the women of the North all a-talking about rights, the white men will be in a fix pretty soon.

But what's all this here talking about? That man over there says that women need to be helped into carriages, and lifted over ditches, and to have the best place everywhere. Nobody ever helps me into carriages, or over mud puddles or gives me any best place *(and raising herself to her full height and her voice to a pitch like rolling thunder, she asked), and* aren't I a woman? Look at me! Look at my arm! *(And she bared her right arm to the shoulder, showing her tremendous muscular power.)* I have plowed, and planted, and gathered into barns, and no man could head me—and aren't I a woman? I could work as much and eat as much as a man (when I could get it), and bear the lash as well—and aren't I a woman? I have borne thirteen children and seen them almost all sold off into slavery, and when I cried out with a mother's grief, none but Jesus heard—and aren't I a woman? Then they talk about this thing in the head—what's this they call it? *("Intellect," whispered someone near.)* That's it honey. What's that got to do with woman's rights or Negroes' rights? If my cup won't hold but a pint and yours holds a quart, wouldn't you be mean not to let me have my little half-measure full? *(And she pointed her significant finger and sent a keen glance at the minister who had made the argument. The cheering was long and loud.)*

Then that little man in black there, he says women can't have as much rights as man, 'cause Christ wasn't a woman. Where

Reprinted with permission from Karlyn Kohrs Campbell, *Key Texts of the Early Feminists*, vol. 2 of *Man Cannot Speak for Her*, Westport, CT: Greenwood Press, 1989.

did your Christ come from? *(Rolling thunder could not have stilled that crowd as did those deep, wonderful tones, as she stood there with outstretched arms and eye of fire. Raising her voice still louder, she repeated,)* Where did your Christ come from? From God and a woman. Man had nothing to do with him. *(Oh! what a rebuke she gave the little man.)*

(Turning again to another objector, she took up the defense of mother Eve. I cannot follower [sic] her through it all. It was pointed, and witty, and solemn, eliciting at almost every sentence deafening applause; and she ended [sic] by asserting that) If the first woman God ever made was strong enough to turn the world upside down, all alone, these together *(and she glanced her eye over us),* ought to be able to turn it back and get it right side up again; and now they are asking to do it, the men better let them. *(Long-continued cheering.)*

'Bliged to you for hearing on me, and now old Sojourner hasn't got anything more to say.

SPEECH DELIVERED TO
THE FIRST ANNUAL MEETING
OF THE AMERICAN EQUAL
RIGHTS ASSOCIATION
(MAY 9, 1867)

M<small>Y FRIENDS, I AM REJOICED THAT YOU ARE GLAD, BUT I DON'T</small>
know how you will feel when I get through. I come from another
field—the country of the slave. They have got their liberty—so
much good luck to have slavery partially destroyed; not entirely.
I want it root and branch destroyed. Then we will all be free indeed. I feel that if I have to answer for the deeds done in my body
just as much as a man, I have a right to have just as much as a
man. There is a great stir about colored men getting their rights,
but not a word about the colored women; and if colored men get
their rights, and not colored women get theirs, you see the colored
men will be masters over the women, and it will be just as bad
as it was before. So I am for keeping the thing going while things
are stirring; because if we wait till it is still, it will take a great
while to get it going again. White women are a great deal smarter,
and know more than colored women, while colored women do
not know scarcely anything. They go out washing, which is about
as high as a colored woman gets, and their men go about idle,
strutting up and down; and when the women come home, they
ask for their money and take it all, and then scold because there
is no food. I want you to consider on that, chil'n. I call you chil'n;
you are somebody's chil'n, and I am old enough to be mother of
all that is here.

I want women to have their rights. In the courts women have
no right, no voice; nobody speaks for them. I wish woman to
have her voice there among the pettifoggers. If it is not a fit place
for women, it is unfit for men to be there.

I am above eighty years old; it is about time for me to be going.
I have been forty years a slave and forty years free, and would be
here forty years more to have equal rights for all. I suppose I am

kept here because something remains for me to do; I suppose I am yet to help break the chain.

I have done a great deal of work; as much as a man, but did not get so much pay. I used to work in the field and bind grain, keeping up with the cradler; but men doing no more, got twice as much pay. So with the German women. They work in the field and do as much work, but do not get the pay. We do as much, we eat as much, we want as much.

I suppose I am about the only colored woman that goes about to speak for the rights of the colored woman. I want to keep the thing stirring, now that the ice is cracked. What we want is a little money. You men know that you get as much again as women when you write, or for what you do. When we get our rights, we shall not have to come to you for money, for then we shall have money enough in our own pockets; and may be you will ask us for money. But help us now until we get it. It is a good consolation to know that when we have got this battle once fought we shall not be coming to you any more.

You have been having our right so long, that you think, like a slave-holder, that you own us. I know that it is hard for one who has held the reins for so long to give up; it cuts like a knife. It will feel all the better when it closes up again. I have been in Washington about three years, seeing about these colored people. Now colored men have a right to vote. There ought to be equal rights more then ever, since colored people have got their freedom.

I am going to talk several times while I am here; so now I will do a little singing. I have not heard any singing since I came here.

(Accordingly, suiting the action to the word, Sojourner sang,) We are going home. There, children, *(said she,)* in heaven we shall rest from all our labors; first do all we have to do here. There I am determined to go, not to stop short of that beautiful place, and I do not mean to stop till I get there, and meet you there, too.

FRANCES ELLEN
3 WATKINS HARPER
(1825–1911)

We are all bound up together in one great bundle of humanity, and society cannot trample on the weakest and feeblest of its members without receiving the curse in its own soul. You tried that in the case of the negro. You pressed him down for two centuries; and in so doing you crippled the moral strength and paralyzed the spiritual energies of the white men of the country.

—Frances Harper, "We Are All Bound Up Together"

IN A LETTER TO WILLIAM STILL, ABOLITIONIST AND AUTHOR OF *The Underground Rail Road*, rhetor Frances Harper described the bonds uniting all of her nineteenth-century audiences. She insisted that "between the white people and the colored there is a community of interests, and the sooner they find it out, the better it will be for both parties" (Still 770). This theme of converging interests prevails in the speeches of Harper, outspoken lecturer, poet, and novelist of the nineteenth century. These converging—and frequently diverging—interests centered on the tensions between women's rights and the rights of newly enfranchised black males, between white women's rights and the rights of black women; between the rights of black males and black females, and between rights of formally educated blacks and the masses of illiterate blacks concentrated in the South.

Born free in Baltimore, Maryland, in 1825, Harper lost her mother when she was three. She was raised by her uncle William Watkins, minister and head of the Watkins' Academy for Negro Youth, where Harper studied the Bible, classical literature, elocution, grammar, mathematics, music, philosophy, reading, and writing. She attended abolitionist meetings with her cousins, who were well known for their oratorical skills. Her uncle frequently contributed articles to such papers as Garrison's *Liberator* and was said to have helped organize a "school of oratory, literature and debate" (qtd. in Foster 7). At the age of thirteen, Harper took a job as a seamstress and nursemaid with the Armstrongs, who owned a bookshop. In her spare time, she read.

At twenty-six, she left Baltimore and began teaching, first in Ohio and later in Pennsylvania. Largely because of an incident involving a free black sold into slavery, Harper gave up teaching to become a lecturer for the abolitionist cause. Her first speech was delivered in New Bedford, Massachusetts, in 1854 at a meeting on the subject the "Education and Elevation of the Colored Race" (Still 758). It has been suggested that the essay "The Colored People of America," appearing in her collection *Poems on Miscellaneous Subjects* (1857), may be the text of this first lecture (Foster 95).

Harper was widely known for her oratorical skills. Journalist Grace Greenwood, calling her the "bronze muse," found it difficult to conceive that Harper might have been "sold on the auction block" and after hearing a series of Harper's lectures in Philadelphia said: "She . . . speaks without notes, with gestures few and fitting. Her manner is marked by dignity and composure. She is never assuming, never theatrical" (Still 779). Mary Ann Shadd Cary, a black abolitionist, journalist, and speaker in her own right, claimed Harper "is the greatest female speaker as ever was here [Detroit]" (Sterling 174). The *Portland Daily Press* described her as having "splendid articulation," using "chaste, pure language," having "a pleasant voice," and allowing "no one to tire of hearing her" (Still 760). These remarks confirm Harper's commanding presence at the lectern.

In 1866, she spoke at the Eleventh National Woman's Rights Convention in New York, the convention at which the AERA was formed. The speech "We Are All Bound Up Together" developed the theme of a community of interests established in earlier speeches and, according to Foster, "marked the beginning of Harper's prominence in national feminist organizations" (216). In this address, she identifies with her audience of women by relating her own experience as a widow. Frances Watkins married Fenton Harper in 1860 at thirty-five. He was a widower with three children; together they had one daughter. After her husband's death four years later, everything was taken from her, not, she stresses, because she was black, but because she was a woman. Her narrative of this experience ends with the proclamation, "I say, then, that justice is not fulfilled so long as woman is unequal before the law," drawing upon the notion that the fate of all humanity is "bound up together" (Harper 46). However, prefiguring her subsequent reservations about a close alliance between black and white women, in this same speech she emphasized points of divergence as well: "I do not believe that giving the woman the ballot is immediately going to cure all the ills of life" (Harper 46). Almost thirty years later, Harper, in "Woman's Political Future," voices these same reservations, again highlighting the tension between women's rights and rights for all people: "I do not think the mere extension of the ballot a panacea for all the ills of our national life. What we need to-day is not simply more voters, but better voters."

Harper delivered "Duty to Dependent Races" in 1891 at the first triennial meeting of the National Council of Women of the United States. Prominent club women organized the council in 1888 during a meeting of the International Council of Women, which Harper had also addressed. Frances Willard and Susan B. Anthony served as first president and vice president. Harper was probably invited because of her prominence as a speaker and her activity in the Woman's Christian Temperance Union, where she served as the only black board member until 1893.[1] The meeting was held at Albaugh's Opera House, with a seating capacity of 2,000, in Washington, D.C. The council *Transactions* list Harper's address under the general subject "Charities and Philanthropies." Other speeches listed under this heading were "State Control of Dependent Classes," "The Care of Dependent Children," "The Need of Women in Public Institutions," and "Women as Police Matrons."

Both Harper and Alice C. Fletcher spoke under the subtopic "Our Duty to Dependent Races." Fletcher, introduced as "a Fellow of the Museum of the Scientific School of Harvard University," defined two "dependent races," the American Indian and the Negro, and addressed the duty her largely white female audience owed to these two races, "each distinct," she says, "from the other, and from our own race, *physiologically and linguistically* [emphasis mine]" (Avery 81). She goes on to address the question, "What shall we from our abundance give to those dependent upon us?" (82). Such was the tenor of the speech Harper's speech followed.

Notice that with her opening sentence in "Duty to Dependent Races," Harper both rejects Fletcher's basic premise that the Negro is dependent, arguing that blacks are simply claiming what is rightfully theirs, and establishes a framework for an alternative view, her *partitio*. Thus the title attributed to this text is misleading, as it suggests that Harper speaks here on the duty of others to provide for the dependent Negro race, when, in fact, she argues not for duties but for rights, and not for a dependent race but for a race entitled to the same rights and privileges as others. These opening remarks establish the speech's refutational tone.

In developing the theme "community of interests," Harper makes several voice shifts. Her opening sentence suggests that she is speaking on the Negro's behalf as a third party (following emphases mine): "*I* deem it a privilege to present *the negro* . . . " and, two paragraphs later, "*I* claim for *the negro* . . . " But, she also identifies with the race when she states, "*Our* first claim upon the nation and government is the claim for protection . . . " When she speaks of the country and its needs, she realigns herself with her audience: "That claim should lie at the basis of *our* civilization, not simply in theory but in fact." And of course in offering advice to her auditors, she turns to the imperative. With these voice shifts Harper places herself in various converging and diverging communities of interest.

"Woman's Political Future," the second speech included here, was delivered in 1893 at the World's Congress of Representative Women. The Congress was held from May 15 to May 22, 1893, in Chicago as part of the Columbian Exposition with the purpose of assessing "the contribution of woman alone to the general progress of society, the reform of social evils, and the bettering of industrial conditions" (Sewall xx). In Harper's address during "The Civil and Political Status of Women" session, she expresses her support for women's rights. However, her arguments are based on what Kraditor, in a discussion of "two major types of suffragist argument," calls expediency rather than justice or natural right, which claimed that women should be allowed to vote because they had the same inherent right as men. The appeal here is to sameness. Elizabeth Cady Stanton and the early suffragists relied primarily on this claim. The argument from expediency, used by some of the later reformers, shifted the focus to difference, claiming that women can bring certain unique maternal attributes to the political table (Kraditor 43–74). Examples of this appeal abound. Harper talks about the "spiritual aid that woman can give for the social advancement and moral development of the human race," and she speaks of woman as the "companion of man." She declares woman's opportunity to fill the world with "fairer and higher aims than the greed of gold and the lust of power" and emphasizes influence as a source of indirect power. As in many of her earlier speeches, she again pulls back from complete endorsement of the vote for women: "I do not believe in unrestricted and universal suffrage for either men or women." In one particularly memorable line from this speech— "If the fifteenth century discovered America to the Old World, the nineteenth is discovering woman to herself"—Harper reflects upon the accomplishments of women near the end of the century, accomplishments that stem more from their moralizing influence than from actual political power.

Margaret Windeyer, an Australian representative who responded to Harper's speech, clearly objected to Harper's notion of women using their influence over men, declaring, "Women have no political present when they do not exercise the franchise. . . . I can not conceive that the underhanded, secret influence which women try to have upon politicians is politics. It is not politics in the best sense; and it is an influence which we ought to do all in our power to remove" (Sewall 437–438). The diverging positions embodied in these speakers highlight the dilemma most women faced as they sought ways to assert their rights. Anna Julia Cooper, too, in an 1886 speech to the Convocation of Colored Clergy (included in this anthology), talks about the influence of women entering public life in "quiet, undisputed dignity." In some respects, Harper's appeal to expediency was indeed expedient, not denying natural right, but, as Kraditor says concerning suffragists at the turn of the century, allowing "new arguments enumerating the reforms that women voters could effect" to take "their places alongside the natural right principle" (45). Harper is not convinced that voting women will necessarily vote the right way. Her concern is more with the character of women so enfranchised and with the kinds of choices they will make. In "Duty to Dependent Races," Harper clearly advocates for the natural right of blacks to exist in this country, but in "Woman's Political Future" she takes a different tack.

Although Harper is best known for her poetry, short fiction, and novel *Iola Leroy,* anecdotal evidence suggests that her speeches also had great impact. Supporting herself primarily with fees earned as a lecturer, Harper spoke to well-established black and white organizations. She gained the respect of their members for her arguments and her delivery. She spoke extensively on plantations in the South to former slaves and slaveholders, in freedmen's schools, and in churches to overflowing crowds. Her oratory rivals that of Frederick Douglass, perhaps the best-known nineteenth-century African-American speaker, in range of occasions, variety of audiences, and years of performance. Both mounted the platform audiences for over fifty years.

NOTE

1. The major black women's organization, the National Association of Colored Women, formed in 1896, did not join the council until 1899.

DUTY TO DEPENDENT RACES
(1891)

W HILE MISS FLETCHER HAS ADVOCATED THE CAUSE OF THE INDIAN and negro under the caption of Dependent races, I deem it a privilege to present the negro, not as a mere dependent asking for Northern sympathy or Southern compassion, but as a member of the body politic who has a claim upon the nation for justice, simple justice, which is the right of every race, upon the government for protection, which is the rightful claim of every citizen, and upon our common Christianity for the best influences which can be exerted for peace on earth and good-will to man.

Our first claim upon the nation and government is the claim for protection to human life. That claim should lie at the basis of our civilization, not simply in theory but in fact. Outside of America, I know of no other civilized country, Catholic, Protestant, or even Mahometan, where men are still lynched, murdered, and even burned for real or supposed crimes. As long as there are such cases as moral irresponsibility, mental imbecility; as long as Potiphar's wife stands in the world's pillory of shame, *no man* should be deprived of life or liberty without due process of law. A government which has power to tax a man in peace, and draft him in war, should have power to defend his life in the hour of peril. A government which can protect and defend its citizens from wrong and outrage and does not is vicious. A government which would do it and cannot is weak; and where human life is insecure through either weakness or viciousness in the administration of law, there must be a lack of justice, and where this is wanting nothing can make up the deficiency.

The strongest nation on earth cannot afford to deal unjustly towards its weakest and feeblest members. A man might just as well attempt to play with the thunderbolts of heaven and expect to escape unscathed, as for a nation to trample on justice and right and evade the divine penalty. The reason our nation snapped asunder in 1861 was because it lacked the cohesion of justice; men poured out their blood like water, scattered their wealth like chaff, summoned to the field the largest armies the nation had ever seen, but they did not get their final victories which closed the rebellion till they clasped hands with the negro, and marched with him abreast to freedom and to victory. I claim for the negro protection in every right with which the government has invested him. Whether it was wise or unwise, the government has exchanged the fetters on his wrist for the ballot in his right hand, and men cannot vitiate his vote by fraud, or intimidate the voter by violence, without being untrue to the genius and spirit of our government, and bringing demoralization into their own political life and ranks. Am I here met with the objection that the negro is poor and ignorant, and the greatest amount of land, capital, and intelligence is possessed by the white race, and that in a number of States negro suffrage means negro supremacy? But is it not a fact that both North and South power naturally gravitates into the strongest hands, and is there any danger that a race who were deemed so inferior as to be only fitted for slavery, and social and political ostracism, has in less than one generation become so powerful that, if not hindered from exercising the right of suffrage, it will dominate over a people who have behind them ages of dominion, education, freedom, and civilization, a people who have had poured into their veins the blood of some of the strongest races on earth? More than a year since Mr. Grady said, I believe, "We do not directly fear the political domination of blacks, but that they are ignorant and easily deluded, impulsive and therefore easily led, strong of race instinct and therefore clannish, without information and therefore without political convictions, passionate and therefore easily excited, poor, irresponsible, and with no idea of the integrity of suffrage and therefore easily bought. The fear is that this vast swarm, ignorant, purchasable, will be impacted and controlled by desperate and unscrupulous white men and made to hold the balance of power when white men are divided." Admit for one moment that every word here is true, and that the whole race should be judged by its worst, and not its best members, does any civilized country legislate to punish a man before he commits a crime?

It is said the negro is ignorant. But why is he ignorant? It comes with ill grace from a man who has put out my eyes to make a parade of my blindness—to reproach me for my poverty when he has wronged me of my money. If the negro is ignorant, he has lived under the shadow of an institution which, at least in part of the country, made it a crime to teach him to read the name of the ever-blessed Christ. If he is poor, what has become of the money he has been earning for the last two hundred and fifty years? Years ago it was said cotton fights and cotton conquers for American slavery. The negro helped build up that great cotton power in the South, and in the North his sigh was in the whir of its machinery, and his blood and tears upon the warp and woof of its manufactures.

But there are some rights more precious than the rights of property or the claims of superior intelligence: they are the rights of life and liberty, and to these the poorest and humblest man has just as much right as the richest and most influential man in the country. Ignorance and poverty are conditions which men outgrow. Since the sealed volume was opened by the crimson hand of war, in spite of entailed ignorance, poverty, opposition, and a heritage of scorn, schools have sprung like wells in the desert dust. It has been estimated that about two millions have learned to read. Colored men and women have gone into journalism. Some of the first magazines in the country have received contributions from them. Learned professions have given them diplomas. Universities have granted them professorships. Colored women have combined to shelter orphaned children. Tens of thousands have been contributed by colored persons for the care of the aged and infirm. Instead of the old slave-pen of former days, imposing and commodious are edifices of prayer and praise. Millions of dollars have flowed into the pockets of the race, and freed people have not only been able to provide for themselves, but reach out their hands to impoverished owners.

Has the record of the slave been such as to warrant the belief that permitting him to share citizenship with others in the country is inimical to the welfare of the nation? Can it be said that he lacks patriotism, or a readiness to make common cause with the nation in the hour of peril? In the days of the American Revolution some of the first blood which was shed flowed from the veins of a colored man, and among the latest words that died upon his lips before they paled in death was, "Crush them underfoot," meaning the British guards. To him Boston has given a monument. In or after 1812 they received from General Jackson the plaudit, "I knew you would endure hunger and thirst and all the hardships of war. I knew that you loved the land of your nativity, and that, like ourselves, you had to defend all that is most dear; but you have surpassed my hopes. I have found in you, united to all these qualities, that noble enthusiasm which impels to great deeds." And in our late civil conflict colored men threw their lives into the struggle, rallied around the old flag when others were trampling it underfoot and riddling it with bullets. Colored people learned to regard that flag as a harbinger of freedom and bring their most reliable information to the Union army, to share their humble fare with the escaping prisoner; to be faithful when others were faithless and help turn the tide of battle in favor of the nation. While nearly two hundred thousand joined the Union army, others remained on the old plantation; widows, wives, aged men, and helpless children were left behind, when the master was at the front trying to put new rivets in their chains, and yet was there a single slave who took advantage of the master's absence to invade the privacy of his home, or wreak a summary vengeance on those whose "defenceless condition should have been their best defence?"

Instead of taking the ballot from his hands, teach him how to use it, and to add his quota to the progress, strength, and durability of the nation. Let the nation, which once consented to his abasement under a system which made it a crime to teach him to read his Bible, feel it a privilege as well as a duty to reverse the old processes of the past by supplanting his darkness with light, not simply by providing the negro, but the whole region in which he lives, with national education. No child can be blamed because he was born in the midst of squalor, poverty, and ignorance, but society is criminal if it permits him to grow up without proper efforts for ameliorating his condition.

Some months since, when I was in South Carolina, where I addressed a number of colored schools, I was informed that white children were in the factories, beginning from eight to ten years old, with working hours from six to seven o'clock; and one day, as a number of white children were wending their way apparently from the factory, I heard a colored man say, "I pity these children." It was a strange turning of the tables to hear a colored man in South Carolina bestowing pity on white children because of neglect in their education. Surely the world does move. When parents are too poor or selfish to spare the labor of their children from the factories, and the State too indifferent or short-sighted to enforce their education by law, then let the Government save its future citizens from the results of cupidity in the parents or short-sightedness in the State. If to-day there is danger from a mass of ignorance voting, may there not be a danger even greater, and that is a mass of "ignorance that does not vote"? If there is danger that an ignorant mass might be compacted to hold the balance of power where white men are divided politically, might not that same mass, if kept ignorant and disfranchised, be used by wicked men, whose weapons may be bombs and dynamite, to dash themselves against the peace and order of society? To-day the hands of the negro are not dripping with dynamite. We do not read of his flaunting the red banners of anarchy in the face of the nation, nor plotting in beer-saloons to overthrow existing institutions, nor spitting on the American flag. Once that flag was to him an ensign of freedom. Let our Government resolve that as far as that flag extends every American-born child shall be able to read upon its folds liberty for all and chains for none.

And now permit me to make my final claim, and that is a claim upon our common Christianity. I believe in the Christianity of the Christ of Calvary, but I cannot believe in all its saddest and most terrible perversions. They are the shadow that has followed its sunshine and hindered its unfulfilled mission. I think of organized Christianity as a stream ploughing through different strata of earth, and partaking of the nature of the soil through which it percolates. It came to Latin races, but its shadow among them was the inquisition devising its tortures and the *auto-da-fé* lighting its fires. It came to Slavic people, and we have the Greek Church with a background of Anti-Semitic persecutions and the horrors of Siberian prisons. Among English-speaking races we have weaker races victimized, a discontented Ireland, and a darkest England. In America we have had an emasculated Christianity,—a Protestantism shorn of protesting strength, which would sing—

Nothing in my hands I bring,
Simply to thy cross I cling,

when it should have brought in its hands the sacrifices of justice
and mercy and broken every yoke and let the oppressed go free.
Degenerate Israel remaining amid the graves, with the host of
abominable things in her vessels, said to those whom she rejected,
"Stand by thyself. Come not near me; I am holier than thou." A
degenerate Christianity sitting by the dishonored tomb of American slavery and remaining amid the graves of the dead past still
virtually says to millions of God's poor children, "Stand by thyself. Come not near me, for I am whiter than thou."
    Underlying this racial question, if I understand it aright, is one
controlling idea, not simply that the negro is ignorant; *that* he is
outgrowing; not that he is incapable of valor in war or adaptation
in peace. On fields all drenched with blood he made his record in
war, abstained from lawless violence when left on the plantation,
and received his freedom in peace with moderation. But he holds
in this Republic the position of an alien race among a people impatient of a rival. And in the eyes of some it seems that no valor
redeems him, no social advancement nor individual development
wipes off the ban which clings to him. It is the pride of Caste
which opposes the spirit of Christ, and the great work to which
American Christianity is called is a work of Christly reconcilia-
tion. God has heaved up your mountains with grandeur, flooded
your rivers with majesty, crowned your vales with fertility, and
enriched your mines with wealth. Excluding Alaska, you have, I
think, nearly three hundred millions of square miles. Be reconciled to God for making a man black, permitting him to become
part of your body politic, and sharing one rood or acre of our
goodly heritage. Be reconciled to the Christ of Calvary, who said,
"And I, if I be lifted up, will draw all men to me," and "It is
better for a man that a millstone were hanged about his neck, and
he were drowned in the depths of the sea, than that he should
offend one of these little ones that believe in me." Forgive the
early adherents of Christianity who faced danger and difficulty
and stood as victors by the side of Death, who would say, "I per-

ceive that God is no respecter of persons." "If ye have respect of persons ye commit sin." "There is neither Greek nor Jew, circumcision nor uncircumcision, Scythian nor Barbarian, bond nor free, but Christ is all, and in all."

What I ask of American Christianity is not to show us more creeds, but more of Christ; not more rites and ceremonies, but more religion glowing with love and replete with life, —religion which will be to all weaker races an uplifting power, and not a degrading influence. Jesus Christ has given us a platform of love and duty from which all oppression and selfishness is necessarily excluded. While politicians may stumble on the barren mountains of fretful controversy and ask in strange bewilderment, "What shall we do with weaker races?" I hold that Jesus Christ answered that question nearly two thousand years since. "Whatsoever ye would that men should do to you, do you even so to them." When His religion fully permeates our civilization, and moulds our national life, the drink traffic will be abolished, the Indian question answered, and the negro problem solved.

WOMAN'S POLITICAL FUTURE
(1893)

IF BEFORE SIN HAD CAST ITS DEEPEST SHADOWS OR SORROW HAD distilled its bitterest tears, it was true that it was not good for man to be alone, it is no less true, since the shadows have deepened and life's sorrows have increased, that the world has need of all the spiritual aid that woman can give for the social advancement and moral development of the human race. The tendency of the present age, with its restlessness, religious upheavals, failures, blunders, and crimes, is toward broader freedom, an increase of knowledge, the emancipation of thought, and a recognition of the brotherhood of man; in this movement woman, as the companion of man, must be a sharer. So close is the bond between man and woman that you can not raise one without lifting the other. The world can not move without woman's sharing in the movement, and to help give a right impetus to that movement is woman's highest privilege.

If the fifteenth century discovered America to the Old World, the nineteenth is discovering woman to herself. Little did Columbus imagine, when the New World broke upon his vision like a lovely gem in the coronet of the universe, the glorious possibilities of a land where the sun should be our engraver, the winged lightning our messenger, and steam our beast of burden. But as mind is more than matter, and the highest ideal always the true real, so to woman comes the opportunity to strive for richer and grander discoveries than ever gladdened the eye of the Genoese mariner.

Not the opportunity of discovering new worlds, but that of filling this old world with fairer and higher aims than the greed of gold and the lust of power, is hers. Through weary, wasting years men have destroyed, dashed in pieces, and overthrown, but to-day we stand on the threshold of woman's era, and woman's work is grandly constructive. In her hand are possibilities whose use or abuse must tell upon the political life of the nation, and send their influence for good or evil across the track of unborn ages.

As the saffron tints and crimson flushes of morn herald the coming day, so the social and political advancement which woman has already gained bears the promise of the rising of the full-orbed sun of emancipation. The result will be not to make home less happy, but society more holy; yet I do not think the mere extension of the ballot a panacea for all the ills of our national life. What we need to-day is not simply more voters, but better voters. To-day there are red-handed men in our republic, who walk unwhipped of justice, who richly deserve to exchange the ballot of the freeman for the wristlets of the felon; brutal and cowardly men, who torture, burn, and lynch their fellow-men, men whose defenselessness should be their best defense and their weakness an ensign of protection. More than the changing of institutions we need the development of a national conscience, and the upbuilding of national character. Men may boast of the aristocracy of blood, may glory in the aristocracy of talent, and be proud of the aristocracy of wealth, but there is one aristocracy which must ever outrank them all, and that is the aristocracy of character; and it is the women of a country who help to mold its character, and to influence if not determine its destiny; and in the political future of our nation woman will not have done what she could if she does not endeavor to have our republic stand foremost among the nations of the earth, wearing sobriety as a crown and righteousness as a garment and a girdle. In coming into her political estate woman will find a mass of illiteracy to be dispelled. If knowledge is power, ignorance is also power. The power that educates wickedness may manipulate and dash against the pillars of any state when they are undermined and honeycombed by injustice.

I envy neither the heart nor the head of any legislator who has been born to an inheritance of privileges, who has behind him ages of education, dominion, civilization, and Christianity, if he stands opposed to the passage of a national education bill, whose purpose is to secure education to the children of those who were born under the shadow of institutions which made it a crime to read.

To-day women hold in their hands influence and opportunity, and with these they have already opened doors which have been closed to others. By opening doors of labor woman has become a rival claimant for at least some of the wealth monopolized by her stronger brother. In the home she is the priestess, in society the queen, in literature she is a power, in legislative halls law-makers have responded to her appeals, and for her sake have humanized and liberalized their laws. The press has felt the impress of her hand. In the pews of the church she constitutes the majority; the pulpit has welcomed her, and in the school she has the blessed privilege of teaching children and youth. To her is apparently coming the added responsibility of political power; and what she now possesses should only be the means of preparing her to use the coming power for the glory of God and the good of mankind; for power without righteousness is one of the most dangerous forces in the world.

Political life in our country has plowed in muddy channels, and needs the infusion of clearer and cleaner waters. I am not sure that women are naturally so much better than men that they will clear the stream by the virtue of their womanhood; it is not through sex but through character that the best influence of women upon the life of the nation must be exerted.

I do not believe in unrestricted and universal suffrage for either men or women. I believe in moral and educational tests. I do not believe that the most ignorant and brutal man is better prepared to add value to the strength and durability of the government than the most cultured, upright, and intelligent woman. I do not think that willful ignorance should swamp earnest intelligence at the ballot-box, nor that educated wickedness, violence, and fraud should cancel the votes of honest men. The unsteady hands of a drunkard can not cast the ballot of a freeman. The hands of lynchers are too red with blood to determine the political character of the government for even four short years. The ballot in the hands of woman means power added to influence. How well she will use that power I can not foretell. Great evils stare us in the face that need to be throttled by the combined power of an upright manhood and an enlightened womanhood; and I know that no nation can gain its full measure of enlightenment and happiness if one-half of it is free and the other half is fettered. China compressed the feet of her women and thereby retarded the steps of her men. The elements of a nation's weakness must ever be found at the hearthstone.

More than the increase of wealth, the power of armies, and the strength of fleets is the need of good homes, of good fathers, and good mothers.

The life of a Roman citizen was in danger in ancient Palestine, and men had bound themselves with a vow that they would eat nothing until they had killed the Apostle Paul. Pagan Rome threw around that imperiled life a bulwark of living clay consisting of four hundred and seventy human hearts, and Paul was saved. Surely the life of the humblest American citizen should be as well protected in America as that of a Roman citizen was in heathen Rome. A wrong done to the weak should be an insult to the strong. Woman coming into her kingdom will find enthroned three great evils, for whose overthrow she should be as strong in a love of justice and humanity as the warrior is in his might. She will find intemperance sending its flood of shame, and death, and sorrow to the homes of men, a fretting leprosy in our politics, and a blighting curse in our social life; the social evil sending to our streets women whose laughter is sadder than their tears, who slide from the paths of sin and shame to the friendly shelter of the grave; and lawlessness enacting in our republic deeds over which angels might weep, if heaven knows sympathy.

How can any woman send petitions to Russia against the horrors of Siberian prisons if, ages after the Inquisition has ceased to devise its tortures, she has not done all she could by influence, tongue, and pen to keep men from making bonfires of the bodies of real or supposed criminals?

O women of America! into your hands God has pressed one of the sublimest opportunities that ever came into the hands of the women of any race or people. It is yours to create a healthy public sentiment; to demand justice, simple justice, as the right of every race; to brand with everlasting infamy the lawless and brutal cowardice that lynches, burns, and tortures your own countrymen.

To grapple with the evils which threaten to undermine the strength of the nation and to lay magazines of powder under the cribs of future generations is no child's play.

Let the hearts of the women of the world respond to the song of the herald angels of peace on earth and good will to men. Let them throb as one heart unified by the grand and holy purpose of uplifting the human race, and humanity will breathe freer, and the world grow brighter. With such a purpose Eden would spring up in our path, and Paradise be around our way.

ANNA JULIA
4 HAYWOOD COOPER
(1858–1964)

All I claim is that there is a feminine as well as a masculine side to truth; that these are related not as inferior and superior, not as better and worse, not as weaker and stronger, but as complements—complements in one necessary and symmetric whole. That as the man is more noble in reason, so the woman is more quick in sympathy. That as he is indefatigable in pursuit of abstract truth, so is she in caring for the interests by the way—striving tenderly and lovingly that not one of the least of these "little ones" should perish.

—Anna Cooper, "The Higher Education of Women"

ANNA JULIA HAYWOOD COOPER WAS BORN IN RALEIGH, NORTH Carolina, on August 10, 1858,[1] to Hannah Stanley Haywood; her father was presumably slaveholder George Washington Haywood (Hutchinson 3). In 1868, she received a scholarship to St. Augustine Normal School, founded by the Board of Missions of the Episcopal church. Even as a teenager, Cooper prevailed against discriminatory practices toward women when she demanded admission into a class in Greek. The teacher was George Cooper, from Nassau in the British West Indies and the second black to be ordained in the Episcopal church in North Carolina. They were married in 1877, when Anna Cooper was eighteen. George Cooper died two years later as a result of what his wife called "hard work and exposure suffered while serving his parish" (qtd. in Shockley 205).

Cooper left St. Augustine in 1881 to pursue additional studies at Oberlin College, obtaining a B.A. in 1884 and awarded the M.A. in 1887. She taught at Wilberforce College in Xenia, Ohio, from 1884 to 1885, then returned to St. Augustine's College, where she remained until 1887. That year Cooper moved to Washington,

D.C., where she accepted a position as math and science teacher at the Washington Colored School, later known as the M Street School and finally Dunbar High School. Cooper served as school principal from 1902 to 1906. Due to a controversy, which some scholars claim stemmed from the DuBois-Booker T. Washington debate over educational preparation for blacks, the D.C. Board of Education declined to reappoint her principal in 1906. Cooper subsequently left Washington to teach at Lincoln Institute in Jefferson City, Missouri. She was reinstated at Dunbar as a Latin teacher four years later by a new superintendent of schools.

During this same period, in 1915, she assumed responsibility for the care of five great-nephews and great-nieces, bringing them from Raleigh to live with her in Washington. She also managed by 1925 to earn a doctoral degree from the University of Paris, becoming, at the age of sixty-seven, the fourth African-American woman to receive the Ph.D.

Upon retiring from public school teaching in 1930, Cooper became second president of Frelinghuysen University, an evening school for working adults. For a while the school operated out of her own home. Cooper devoted her remaining years to this institution until her death in 1964.

In addition to being an educator and author, Cooper was an outspoken "race woman," a term applied in the nineteenth century to prominent black women active in the struggle for racial uplift and was also in the vanguard of the black women's club movement. She helped to organize the Colored Women's League in Washington in 1892. Cooper also published a collection of her speeches and essays, *A Voice from the South by a Black Woman of the South*, that year. In 1893, following Fannie Barrier Williams's major address to the World's Congress of Representative Women in Chicago (included in this anthology), Cooper made brief remarks regarding the progress of black women. She recalled their "heroic struggle, a struggle against fearful and overwhelming odds, that often ended in a horrible death, to maintain and protect that which woman holds dearer than life" (Sewall 711). She attended the First Congress of Colored Women in Boston in 1895. On the strength of her intellectual activities, Cooper was the only woman selected for membership in the American Negro Academy, founded

by Alexander Crummell, a black Episcopalian priest. In 1900, she
was one of only a few black women to speak at the Pan-African
Conference in London.

In 1886, a year before she moved to Washington, Cooper was
invited there to deliver the speech "Womanhood a Vital Element
in the Regeneration and Progress of a Race" to the Convocation of
Clergy of the Protestant Episcopal Church. Twenty-seven years
old at the time, she was the guest of Alexander Crummell and
may have delivered this speech at St. Luke's Episcopal Church,
from which Crummell had recently retired to become pastor emeri-
tus. In December of 1884, Cooper had been guest speaker at a
reception on the occasion of his retirement. At that time, she
praised his defense of the Southern black woman as she did again
in "Womanhood a Vital Element" (Moses 242).

The speech resonates with the rhetoric of the classroom. Her
teacherly commentary constantly guides and orients her audience of Episcopalian clergy. Such expressions as, "It is pleasing
to turn from . . . to . . ."; "And here let me say parenthetically
that . . . "; "Now let us see on what basis this hope for our country . . . rests"; "It may help us . . . to recall . . . ," along with the
general use of the first person plural, join audience and rhetor in
a collectively instructive endeavor. Allusions to such famous intellectuals as Madame de Stael, Emerson, Tacitus, Macaulay, and
Wordsworth heighten the speech's scholarly tone.

As an extension of this tone, her metaphors invoke comparison
to plant life and images of growth and development. These metaphors appear most often in Cooper's description of the Southern
black woman in relation to the race: "A race cannot be purified
from without. Preachers and teachers are helps, and stimulants
and conditions as necessary as the gracious rain and sunshine are
to plant growth. But what are rain and dew and sunshine and
cloud if there be no life in the plant germ? We must go to the root
and see that that is sound and healthy and vigorous; and not deceive ourselves with waxen flowers and painted leaves of mock
chlorophyll." This imagery prevails throughout the speech and
is, no doubt, a reflection of her own conviction that progress is
growth.

Cooper's message is that women play a vital role in the advancement of a people. After an opening section of several paragraphs on women's treatment throughout history, Cooper establishes its relevance for her auditors: "Now the fact of woman's influence on society being granted, what are its practical bearings on the work which brought together this conference of colored clergy and laymen in Washington?" She acknowledges some difficulty in developing the assigned speech topic, "woman's influence on social progress," citing her belief that it should be apparent. But she later claims that such influence was a woman's greatest source of power, especially the black woman's.

Her thesis is that before race problems can be solved effectively, all must collectively work for the improvement of the black woman, and particularly for the Southern black woman, only two decades beyond enslavement. Instead of singing the praises of those who have managed to achieve, to earn degrees and high positions, she stresses the need to cultivate and advance those most influential in shaping young minds by virtue of their positions as homemakers and mothers—women. Her appeal for the improvement of the conditions of women is based on what Kraditor calls the suffrage argument from expediency, though Cooper here makes no direct mention of voting rights.[2] In the famous line "Only the BLACK WOMAN can say 'when and where I enter, in the quiet, undisputed dignity of my womanhood, without violence and without suing or special patronage, then and there the whole Negro race enters with me,' " she claims a separate sphere for women. The argument here is from difference, not sameness or natural right. You need women, she tells the clergymen, because of their unique womanly attributes.

Historian Ellen DuBois, referring to women from an earlier period, also comments on the inability of many feminists to confront a certain "contradiction in their feminism." She claims that those who argued for women's equality often ignored the fact that women were dependent on men and confined to the home. Believing that women were naturally suited for domestic activities, these early feminists failed to advocate a complete household reorganization (DuBois 37). Cooper, in her address to the Episcopalian clergy, makes a stronger plea for special treatment than for equal treatment.

Mary Helen Washington, in her introduction to Cooper's *Voice from the South*, comments on the tension between Cooper's identification with "ordinary black working women" and her own reserved intellectualism. In her view, while Cooper clearly voices the concerns of Southern black women, she never considers them her peers (xxx). This Janus-like posture was maintained by many of the women included in this collection. Like Cooper, Maria Stewart, Fannie Barrier Williams, Ida Wells, Frances Harper, and Victoria Matthews were all intellectuals who were either born free or released from slavery when quite young. Yet they all mounted the platform to represent their sisters, regardless of immediate shared experience. "To counteract the prevailing assumptions about black women as immoral and ignorant," Washington says, "Cooper had to construct a narrator who was aware of the plight of uneducated women but was clearly set apart from them in refinement, intelligence, and training" (xxx).

In the second half of Cooper's speech, she directs her attacks specifically against the Episcopalian church, of which she was a member, and its ministry in the South. This charge to be relevant to the needs of the community reverberates from pulpits today as the black church of the 1990s struggles to assert itself as a significant force. With a surprising tone of denominational elitism, she implies that the Episcopalian church, with its "quiet, chaste dignity and decorous solemnity," is best suited to temper the "rank exuberance and often ludicrous demonstrativeness" of the Southern black Christian and expresses regret that other denominations have led the way in attracting members. In particular, Cooper challenges the black clergy in her audience to become more intentional in their efforts to assist the black woman, who, after all, is the strongest influence on the emerging race. One reason she offers for the failure of her church to reach out to the masses is that it has not been aggressively aiding the black woman's development.

After this strong criticism, Cooper comes round to her central point: no denomination can thrive without nurturing its women, not even the Episcopalian. As Cooper, only twenty-seven years old, addresses the group of ministers, all probably considerably older, about their sins of omission, she appeals to their intellect, their religious training, and their sense of duty to their race for particular help for the black woman of the South. Cooper herself identifies with her Episcopalian audience, even as she condemns their neglect.

The text is from Cooper's collection, *A Voice from the South* (1892). I have inserted a few explanatory notes and have incorporated Cooper's own notes as indicated.

NOTES

1. Some sources cite 1859 as the year of her birth (e.g., Shockley 204; Harley 87). Hutchinson cites 1858 as "the probable year of Anna's birth" (14); Loewenberg and Bogin also cite 1858.

2. See discussion of Kraditor's types of suffrage arguments in the introduction to Frances Harper's speeches.

WOMANHOOD A VITAL ELEMENT IN THE REGENERATION AND PROGRESS OF A RACE
(1886)

THE TWO SOURCES FROM WHICH, PERHAPS, MODERN CIVILIZATION
has derived its noble and ennobling ideal of woman are Christianity and the Feudal System.

In Oriental countries woman has been uniformly devoted to a
life of ignorance, infamy, and complete stagnation. The Chinese
shoe of today does not more entirely dwarf, cramp, and destroy
her physical powers, than have the customs, laws, and social instincts, which from remotest ages have governed our Sister of the
East, enervated and blighted her mental and moral life.

Mahomet makes no account of woman whatever in his polity.
The Koran, which, unlike our Bible, was a product and not a
growth, tried to address itself to the needs of Arabian civilization
as Mahomet with his circumscribed powers saw them. The Arab
was a nomad. Home to him meant his present camping place.
That deity who, according to our western ideals, makes and sanctifies the home, was to him a transient bauble to be toyed with
so long as it gave pleasure and then to be thrown aside for a new
one. As a personality, an individual soul, capable of eternal growth
and unlimited development, and destined to mould and shape the
civilization of the future to an incalculable extent Mahomet did
not know woman. There was no hereafter, no paradise for her.
The heaven of the Mussulman is peopled and made gladsome not
by the departed wife, or sister, or mother, but by houri—a figment of Mahomet's brain, partaking of the ethereal qualities of
angels, yet imbued with all the vices and inanity of Oriental women.
The harem here, and "dust to dust" hereafter, this was the hope,
the inspiration, the summum bonum of the Eastern woman's
life! With what result on the life of the nation, the "Unspeakable
Turk," the "sick man" of modern Europe can today exemplify.

Says a certain writer: "The private life of the Turk is vilest
of the vile, unprogressive, unambitious, and inconceivably low."
And yet Turkey is not without her great men. She has produced

53

most brilliant minds; men skilled in all the intricacies of diplomacy and statesmanship; men whose intellects could grapple with the deep problems of empire and manipulate the subtle agencies which check-mate kings. But these minds were not the normal outgrowth of a healthy trunk. They seemed rather ephemeral excrescencies which shoot far out with all the vigor and promise, apparently, of strong branches; but soon alas fall into decay and ugliness because there is no soundness in the root, no life-giving sap, permeating, strengthening and perpetuating the whole. There is a worm at the core! The homelife is impure! and when we look for fruit, like apples of Sodom, it crumbles within our grasp into dust and ashes.

It is pleasing to turn from this effete and immobile civilization to a society still fresh and vigorous whose seed is in itself, and whose very name is synonymous with all that is progressive, elevating and inspiring, viz., the European bud and the American flower of modern civilization.

And here let me say parenthetically that our satisfaction in American institutions rests not on the fruition we now enjoy, but springs rather from the possibilities and promise that are inherent in the system, though as yet, perhaps, far in the future.

"Happiness," says Madame de Staël, "consists not in perfections attained, but in a sense of progress, the result of our own endeavor under conspiring circumstances toward a goal which continually advances and broadens and deepens till it is swallowed up in the Infinite."[1] Such conditions in embryo are all that we claim for the land of the West. We have not yet reached our ideal in American civilization. The pessimists even declare that we are not marching in that direction. But there can be no doubt that here in America is the arena in which the next triumph of civilization is to be won; and here too we find promise abundant and possibilities infinite.

Now let us see on what basis this hope for our country primarily and fundamentally rests. Can any one doubt that it is chiefly on the homelife and on the influence of good women in those

---

1. Madame de Staël (1776–1817) was a French novelist, critic, and literary patron.

homes? Says Macaulay: "You may judge a nation's rank in the scale of civilization from the way they treat their women."[2] And Emerson, "I have thought that a sufficient measure of civilization is the influence of good women." Now this high regard for woman, this germ of a prolific idea which in our own day is bearing such rich and varied fruit, was ingrafted into European civilization, we have said, from two sources, the Christian Church and the Feudal System. For although the Feudal System can in no sense be said to have originated the idea, yet there can be no doubt that the habits of life and modes of thought to which Feudalism gave rise, materially fostered and developed it; for they gave us chivalry, than [sic that] which no institution has more sensibly magnified[,] and elevated woman's position in society.

Tacitus dwells on the tender regard for woman entertained by these rugged barbarians before they left their northern homes to overrun Europe.[3] Old Norse legends too, and primitive poems, all breathe the same spirit of love of home and veneration for the pure and noble influence there presiding—the wife, the sister, the mother.

And when later on we see the settled life of the Middle Ages "oozing out," as M. Guizot expresses it, from the plundering and pillaging life of barbarism and crystallizing into the Feudal System, the tiger of the field is brought once more within the charmed circle of the goddesses of his castle, and his imagination weaves around them a halo whose reflection possibly has not yet altogether vanished.[4]

It is true the spirit of Christianity had not yet put the seal of catholicity on this sentiment. Chivalry, according to Bascom, was but the toning down and softening of a rough and lawless period.[5] It gave a roseate glow to a bitter winter's day. Those who looked out from castle windows revelled in its "amethyst tints." But God's poor, the weak, the unlovely, the commonplace were

2. Thomas Babington Macaulay (1800–1859) was an English historian.
3. Cornelius Tacitus (c. 55–c. 120) was a Roman historian.
4. François-Pierre Guillaume Guizot (1787–1874) was a French historian and statesman.
5. John Bascom (1827–1911) was an American author and professor of rhetoric, oratory, and philosophy.

still freezing and starving none the less in unpitied, unrelieved loneliness.

Respect for woman, the much lauded chivalry of the Middle Ages, meant what I fear it still means to some men in our own day—respect for the elect few among whom they expect to consort.

The idea of the radical amelioration of womankind, reverence for woman as woman regardless of rank, wealth, or culture, was to come from that rich and bounteous fountain from which flow all our liberal and universal ideas—the Gospel of Jesus Christ.

And yet the Christian Church at the time of which we have been speaking would seem to have been doing even less to protect and elevate woman than the little done by secular society. The Church as an organization committed a double offense against woman in the Middle Ages. Making of marriage a sacrament and at the same time insisting on the celibacy of the clergy and other religious orders, she gave an inferior if not an impure character to the marriage relation, especially fitted to reflect discredit on woman. Would this were all or the worst! but the Church by the licentiousness of its chosen servants invaded the household and established too often as vicious connections those relations which it forbade to assume openly and in good faith. "Thus," to use the words of our authority, "the religious corps became as numerous, as searching, and as unclean as the frogs of Egypt, which penetrated into all quarters, into the ovens and kneading troughs, leaving their filthy trail wherever they went." Says Chaucer with characteristic satire, speaking of the Friars:

> Women may now go safely up and doun,
> In every bush, and under every tree,
> Ther is non other incubus but he,
> And he ne will don hem no dishonour.

Henry, Bishop of Liege, could unblushingly boast the birth of twenty-two children in fourteen years.[6]

It may help us under some of the perplexities which beset our

6. Cooper cites Bascom as her source here.

way in "the one Catholic and Apostolic Church" to-day, to recall
some of the corruptions and incongruities against which the Bride
of Christ has had to struggle in her past history and in spite of
which she has kept, through many vicissitudes, the faith once delivered to the saints. Individuals, organizations, whole sections of
the Church militant may outrage the Christ whom they profess,
may ruthlessly trample under foot both the spirit and the letter of
his precepts, yet not till we hear the voices audibly saying "Come
let us depart hence," shall we cease to believe and cling to the
promise, "I am with you to the end of the world."

> Yet saints their watch are keeping,
> The cry goes up "How long!"
> And soon the night of weeping
> Shall be the morn of song.

However much then the facts of any particular period of history
may seem to deny it, I for one do not doubt that the source of
the vitalizing principle of woman's development and amelioration
is the Christian Church, so far as that church is coincident with
Christianity.

Christ gave ideals not formulae. The Gospel is a germ requiring
millennia for its growth and ripening. It needs and at the same
time helps to form around itself a soil enriched in civilization, and
perfected in culture and insight without which the embryo can
neither be unfolded or comprehended. With all the strides our
civilization has made from the first to the nineteenth century, we
can boast not an idea, not a principle of action, not a progressive
social force but was already mutely foreshadowed, or directly en-
joined in that simple tale of a meek and lowly life. The quiet face
of the Nazarene is ever seen a little way ahead, never too far to
come down to and touch the life of the lowest in days the darkest,
yet ever leading onward, still onward, the tottering childish feet
of our strangely boastful civilization.

By laying down for woman the same code of morality, the same
standard of purity, as for man; by refusing to countenance the
shameless and equally guilty monsters who were gloating over
her fall,—graciously stooping in all the majesty of his own spot-

lessness to wipe away the filth and grime of her guilty past and bid her go in peace and sin no more; and again in the moments of his own careworn and footsore dejection, turning trustfully and lovingly, away from the heartless snubbing and sneers, away from the cruel malignity of mobs and prelates in the dusty marts of Jerusalem to the ready sympathy, loving appreciation and un-faltering friendship of that quiet home at Bethany; and even at the last, by his dying bequest to the disciple whom he loved, signi-fying the protection and tender regard to be extended to that sor-rowing mother and ever afterward to the sex she represented;— throughout his life and in his death he has given to men a rule and guide for the estimation of woman as an equal, as a helper, as a friend, and as a sacred charge to be sheltered and cared for with a brother's love and sympathy, lessons which nineteen cen-turies' gigantic strides in knowledge, arts, and sciences, in social and ethical principles have not been able to probe to their depth or to exhaust in practice.

It seems not too much to say then of the vitalizing, regenerat-ing, and progressive influence of womanhood on the civilization of to-day, that, while it was foreshadowed among Germanic na-tions in the far away dawn of their history as a narrow, sickly and stunted growth, it yet owes its catholicity and power, the deep-ening of its roots and broadening of its branches to Christianity.

The union of these two forces, the Barbaric and the Christian, was not long delayed after the Fall of the Empire. The Church, which fell with Rome, finding herself in danger of being swal-lowed up by barbarism, with characteristic vigor and fertility of resources, addressed herself immediately to the task of con-quering her conquerers [*sic*]. The means chosen does credit to her power of penetration and adaptability, as well as to her profound, unerring, all-compassing diplomacy; and makes us even now won-der if aught human can successfully and ultimately withstand her far-seeing designs and brilliant policy, or gainsay her well-earned claim to the word Catholic.

She saw the barbarian, little more developed than a wild beast. She forbore to antagonize and mystify his warlike nature by a full blaze of the heartsearching and humanizing tenets of her great Head. She said little of the rule "If thy brother smite thee on one

cheek, turn to him the other also;" but thought it sufficient for
the needs of those times, to establish the so-called "Truce Of
God" under which men were bound to abstain from butchering
one another for three days of each week and on Church festivals.
In other words, she respected their individuality: non-resistance
pure and simple being for them an utter impossibility, she con-
tented herself with less radical measures calculated to lead up finally to the full measure of the benevolence of Christ.

Next she took advantage of the barbarian's sensuous love of
gaudy display and put all her magnificent garments on. She could
not capture him by physical force, she would dazzle him by gor-
geous spectacles. It is said that Romanism gained more in pomp
and ritual during this trying period of the Dark Ages than throughout all her former history.

The result was she carried her point. Once more Rome laid her
ambitious hand on the temporal power, and allied with Charle-
magne, aspired to rule the world through a civilization dominated
by Christianity and permeated by the traditions and instincts of
those sturdy barbarians.

Here was the confluence of the two streams we have been trac-
ing, which, united now, stretch before us as a broad majestic river.
In regard to woman it was the meeting of two noble and ennobling forces, two kindred ideas the resultant of which, we doubt
not, is destined to be a potent force in the betterment of the world.

Now after our appeal to history comparing nations destitute
of this force and so destitute also of principle of progress, with
other nations among whom the influence of woman is prominent
coupled with a brisk, progressive, satisfying civilization,—if in
addition we find this strong presumptive evidence corroborated
by reason and experience, we may conclude that these two equally
varying concomitants are linked as cause and effect; in other words,
that the position of woman in society determines the vital elements of its regeneration and progress.

Now that this is so on a priori grounds all must admit. And
this not because woman is better or stronger or wiser than man,
but from the nature of the case, because it is she who must first
form the man by directing the earliest impulses of his character.

Byron and Wordsworth were both geniuses and would have

stamped themselves on the thought of their age under any circumstances; and yet we find the one a savor of life unto life, the
other of death unto death. "Byron, like a rocket, shot his way
upward with scorn and repulsion, flamed out in wild, explosive,
brilliant excesses and disappeared in darkness made all the more
palpable."[7]
Wordsworth lent of his gifts to reinforce that "power in the
Universe which makes for righteousness" by taking the harp handed
him from Heaven and using it to swell the strains of angelic choirs.
Two locomotives equally mighty stand facing opposite tracks; the
one to rush headlong to destruction with all its precious freight,
the other to toil grandly and gloriously up the steep embattle-
ments to Heaven and to God. Who—who can say what a world
of consequences hung on the first placing and starting of these
enormous forces!
Woman, Mother,—your responsibility is one that might make
angels tremble and fear to take hold! To trifle with it, to ignore
or misuse it, is to treat lightly the most sacred and solemn trust
ever confided by God to human kind. The training of children is
a task on which an infinity of weal or woe depends. Who does
not covet it? Yet who does not stand awe-struck before its momentous issues! It is a matter of small moment, it seems to me,
whether that lovely girl in whose accomplishments you take such
pride and delight, can enter the gay and crowded salon with the
ease and elegance of this or that French or English gentlewoman,
compared with the decision as to whether her individuality is
going to reinforce the good or the evil elements of the world. The
lace and the diamonds, the dance and the theater, gain a new significance when scanned in their bearings on such issues. Their
influence on the individual personality, and through her on the
society and civilization which she vitalizes and inspires—all this
and more must be weighed in the balance before the jury can return a just and intelligent verdict as to the innocence or baneful-
ness of these apparently simple amusements.
Now the fact of woman's influence on society being granted,

7. Cooper cites "Bascom's Engl. Lit. p. 253" as the source for this
quote (probably Bascom's *Philosophy of English Literature*, 1874).

what are its practical bearings on the work which brought together this conference of colored clergy and laymen in Washington? "We come not here to talk." Life is too busy, too pregnant
with meaning and far reaching consequences to allow you to come
this far for mere intellectual entertainment.

The vital agency of womanhood in the regeneration and progress of a race, as a general question, is conceded almost before it
is fairly stated. I confess one of the difficulties for me in the subject
assigned lay in its obviousness. The plea is taken away by the opposite attorney's granting the whole question.

"Woman's influence on social progress"—who in Christen-
dom doubts or questions it? One may as well be called on to prove
that the sun is the source of light and heat and energy to this
many-sided little world.

Nor, on the other hand, could it have been intended that I should
apply the position when taken and proven, to the needs and responsibilities of the women of our race in the South. For is it
not written, "Cursed is he that cometh after the king?" and has
not the King already preceded me in "The Black Woman of the
South"?[8]

They have had both Moses and the Prophets in Dr. Crummell
and if they hear not him, neither would they be persuaded though
one came up from the South.

I would beg, however, with the Doctor's permission, to add
my plea for the Colored Girls of the South: that large, bright,
promising fatally beautiful class that stand shivering like a delicate
plantlet before the fury of tempestuous elements, so full of promise and possibilities, yet so sure of destruction; often without a
father to whom they dare apply the loving term, often without a
stronger brother to espouse their cause and defend their honor
with his life's blood; in the midst of pitfalls and snares, waylaid
by the lower classes of white men, with no shelter, no protec-

---

8. "The Black Woman of the South: Her Neglects and Her Needs"
was perhaps the best-known sociological essay by Alexander Crummell
(see introductory notes). "It was printed in an edition of 500,000 copies
and is said to have generated over one million dollars for the Freedman's
Aid Society, the organization before which it originally had been delivered and which sponsored its publication" (Moses 298).

tion nearer than the great blue vault above, which half conceals
and half reveals the one Care-Taker they know so little of. Oh,
save them, help them, shield, train, develop, teach, inspire them!
Snatch them, in God's name, as brands from the burning! There
is material in them well worth your while, the hope in germ of a
staunch, helpful, regenerating womanhood on which, primarily,
rests the foundation stones of our future as a race.

It is absurd to quote statistics showing the Negro's bank account and rent rolls, to point to the hundreds of newspapers edited
by colored men and lists of lawyers, doctors, professors, D.D.'s,
LL.D.'s, etc., etc., etc., while the source from which the life-
blood of the race is to flow is subject to taint and corruption in
the enemy's camp.

True progress is never made by spasms. Real progress is growth.
It must begin in the seed. Then, "first the blade, then the ear,
after that the full corn in the ear." There is something to encourage
and inspire us in the advancement of individuals since their emancipation from slavery. It at least proves that there is nothing irre-
trievably wrong in the shape of the black man's skull, and that
under given circumstances his development, downward or upward, will be similar to that of other average human beings.

But there is no time to be wasted in mere felicitation. That the
Negro has his niche in the infinite purposes of the Eternal, no
one who has studied the history of the last fifty years in America
will deny. That much depends on his own right comprehension
of his responsibility and rising to the demands of the hour, it will
be good for him to see; and how best to use his present so that the
structure of the future shall be stronger and higher and brighter
and nobler and holier than that of the past, is a question to be
decided each day by every one of us.

The race is just twenty-one years removed from the conception
and experience of a chattel, just at the age of ruddy manhood. It
is well enough to pause a moment for retrospection, introspec-
tion, and prospection. We look back, not to become inflated with
conceit because of the depths from which we have arisen, but that
we may learn wisdom from experience. We look within that we
may gather together once more our forces, and, by improved and
more practical methods, address ourselves to the tasks before us.

We look forward with hope and trust that the same God whose guiding hand led our fathers through and out of the gall and bitterness of oppression, will still lead and direct their children, to the honor of His name, and for their ultimate salvation.

But this survey of the failures or achievements of the past, the difficulties and embarrassments of the present, and the mingled hopes and fears for the future, must not degenerate into mere dreaming nor consume the time which belongs to the practical and effective handling of the crucial questions of the hour; and there can be no issue more vital and momentous than this of the womanhood of the race.

Here is the vulnerable point, not in the heel, but at the heart of the young Achilles; and here must the defenses be strengthened and the watch redoubled.

We are the heirs of a past which was not our fathers' moulding. "Every man the arbiter of his own destiny" was not true for the American Negro of the past: and it is no fault of his that he finds himself to-day the inheritor of a manhood and womanhood impoverished and debased by two centuries and more of compression and degradation.

But weaknesses and malformations, which to-day are attributable to a vicious schoolmaster and a pernicious system, will a century hence be rightly regarded as proofs of innate corruptness and radical incurability.

Now the fundamental agency under God in the regeneration, the re-training of the race, as well as the ground work and starting point of its progress upward, must be the black woman.

With all the wrongs and neglects of her past, with all the weakness, the debasement, the moral thralldom of her present, the black woman of to-day stands mute and wondering at the Herculean task devolving upon her. But the cycles wait for her. No other hand can move the lever. She must be loosed from her bands and set to work.

Our meager and superficial results from past efforts prove their futility; and every attempt to elevate the Negro, whether undertaken by himself or through the philanthropy of others, cannot but prove abortive unless so directed as to utilize the indispensable agency of an elevated and trained womanhood.

A race cannot be purified from without. Preachers and teachers are helps, and stimulants and conditions as necessary as the gracious rain and sunshine are to plant growth. But what are rain and dew and sunshine and cloud if there be no life in the plant germ? We must go to the root and see that that is sound and healthy and vigorous; and not deceive ourselves with waxen flowers and painted leaves of mock chlorophyll.

We too often mistake individuals' honor for race development and so are ready to substitute pretty accomplishments for sound sense and earnest purpose.

A stream cannot rise higher than its source. The atmosphere of homes is no rarer and purer and sweeter than are the mothers in those homes. A race is but a total of families. The nation is the aggregate of its homes. As the whole is sum of all its parts, so the character of the parts will determine the characteristics of the whole. These are all axioms and so evident that it seems gratuitous to remark it; and yet, unless I am greatly mistaken, most of the unsatisfaction from our past results arises from just such a radical and palpable error as much almost on our own part as on that of our benevolent white friends.

The Negro is constitutionally hopeful and proverbially irrepressible; and naturally stands in danger of being dazzled by the shimmer and tinsel of superficials. We often mistake foliage for fruit and overestimate or wrongly estimate brilliant results.

The late Martin R. Delany, who was an unadulterated black man, used to say when honors of state fell upon him, that when he entered the council of kings the black race entered with him; meaning, I suppose, that there was no discounting his race identity and attributing his achievements to some admixture of Saxon blood.[9] But our present record of eminent men, when placed beside the actual status of the race in America to-day, proves that no man can represent the race. Whatever the attainments of the individual may be, unless his home has moved on pari passu, he can never be regarded as identical with or representative of the whole.

9. Martin R. Delany (1812–1885) was a physician, journalist, emigrationist, and novelist (*Blake or The Huts of America, 1859*).

Not by pointing to sun-bathed mountain tops do we prove that Phoebus warms the valleys. We must point to homes, average homes, homes of the rank and file of horny handed toiling men and women of the South (where the masses are) lighted and cheered by the good, the beautiful, and the true, then and not till then— will the whole plateau be lifted into the sunlight.

Only the BLACK WOMAN can say "when and where I enter, in the quiet, undisputed dignity of my womanhood, without violence and without suing or special patronage, then and there the whole Negro race enters with me." Is it not evident then that as individual workers for this race we must address ourselves with no half-hearted zeal to this feature of our mission. The need is felt and must be recognized by all. There is a call for workers, for missionaries, for men and women with the double consecration of a fundamental love of humanity and a desire for its melioration through the Gospel; but superadded to this we demand an intelligent and sympathetic comprehension of the interests and special needs of the Negro.

I see not why there should not be an organized effort for the protection and elevation of our girls such as the White Cross League in England. English women are strengthened and protected by more than twelve centuries of Christian influences, freedom and civilization; English girls are dispirited and crushed down by no such all-levelling prejudice as that supercilious caste spirit in America which cynically assumes "A Negro woman cannot be a lady." English womanhood is beset by no such snares and traps as betray the unprotected, untrained colored girl of the South, whose only crime and dire destruction often is her unconscious and marvelous beauty. Surely then if English indignation is aroused and English manhood thrilled under the leadership of a Bishop of the English church to build up bulwarks around their wronged sisters, Negro sentiment cannot remain callous and Negro effort nerveless in view of the imminent peril of the mothers of the next generation. "I am my Sister's keeper!" should be the hearty response of every man and woman of the race, and this conviction should purify and exalt the narrow, selfish and petty personal aims of life into a noble and sacred purpose.

We need men who can let their interest and gallantry extend

outside the circle of their aesthetic appreciation; men who can be a father, a brother, a friend to every weak, struggling unshielded girl. We need women who are so sure of their own social footing that they need not fear leaning to lend a hand to a fallen or falling sister. We need men and women who do not exhaust their genius splitting hairs on aristocratic distinctions and thanking God they are not as others; but earnest, unselfish souls, who can go into the highways and byways, lifting up and leading, advising and encouraging with the truly catholic benevolence of the Gospel of Christ.

As Church workers we must confess our path of duty is less obvious; or rather our ability to adapt our machinery to our conception of the peculiar exigencies of this work as taught by experience and our own consciousness of the needs of the Negro, is as yet not demonstrable. Flexibility and aggressiveness are not such strong characteristics of the Church to-day as in the Dark Ages.

As a Mission field for the Church the Southern Negro is in some aspects most promising; in others, perplexing. Aliens neither in language and customs, nor in associations and sympathies, naturally of deeply rooted religious instincts and taking most readily and kindly to the worship and teachings of the Church, surely the task of proselytizing the American Negro is infinitely less formidable than that which confronted the Church in the Barbarians of Europe. Besides, this people already look to the Church as the hope of their race. Thinking colored men almost uniformly admit that the Protestant Episcopal Church with its quiet, chaste dignity and decorous solemnity, its instructive and elevating ritual, its bright chanting and joyous hymning, is eminently fitted to correct the peculiar faults of worship—the rank exuberance and often ludicrous demonstrativeness of their people. Yet, strange to say, the Church, claiming to be missionary and Catholic, urging that schism is sin and denominationalism inexcusable, has made in all these years almost no inroads upon this semi-civilized religionism.

Harvests from this over ripe field of home missions have been gathered in by Methodists, Baptists, and not least by Congregationalists, who were unknown to the Freedmen before their emancipation.

Our clergy numbers less than two dozen priests of Negro blood and we have hardly more than one self-supporting colored congregation in the entire Southland.[10] While the organization known as the A.M.E. Church has 14,063 ministers itinerant and local, 4,069 self-supporting churches, 4,275 Sunday-schools, with property valued at $7,772,284, raising yearly for church purposes $1,427,000.

Stranger and more significant than all, the leading men of this race (I do not mean demagogues and politicians, but men of intellect, heart, and race devotion, men to whom the elevation of their people means more than personal ambition and sordid gain— and the men of that stamp have not all died yet) the Christian workers for the race, of younger and more cultured growth, are noticeably drifting into sectarian churches, many of them declaring all the time that they acknowledge the historic claims of the Church, believe her apostolicity, and would experience greater personal comfort, spiritual and intellectual, in her revered communion. It is a fact which any one may verify for himself, that representative colored men, professing that in their heart of hearts they are Episcopalians, are actually working in Methodist and Baptist pulpits; while the ranks of the Episcopal clergy are left to be filled largely by men who certainly suggest the propriety of a "perpetual Diaconate" if they cannot be said to have created the necessity for it.

Now where is the trouble? Something must be wrong. What is it?

A certain Southern Bishop of our Church reviewing the situation, whether in Godly anxiety or in "Gothic antipathy" I know not, deprecates the fact that the colored people do not seem drawn to the Episcopal Church, and comes to the sage conclusion that

10. Cooper's note: "The published report of '91 shows 26 priests for the entire country, including one not engaged in work and one a professor in a non-sectarian school, since made Dean of an Episcopal Annex to Howard University known as King Hall."

the Church is not adapted to the rude untutored minds of the
Freedmen, and that they may be left to go to the Methodists and
Baptists whither their racial proclivities undeniably tend. How
the good Bishop can agree that all-foreseeing Wisdom, and Catholic Love would have framed his Church as typified in his seamless
garment and unbroken body, and yet not leave it broad enough
and deep enough and loving enough to seek and save and hold
seven millions of God's poor, I cannot see.

But the doctors while discussing their scientifically conclusive
diagnosis of the disease, will perhaps not think it presumptuous
in the patient if he dares to suggest where at least the pain is. If
this be allowed, a Black woman of the South would beg to point
out two possible oversights in this southern work which may in-
dicate in part both a cause and a remedy for some failure. The
first is not calculating for the Black man's personality; not having
respect, if I may so express it, to his manhood or deterring at all
to his conceptions of the needs of his people. When colored persons have been employed it was too often as machines or as mani-
kins. There has been no disposition, generally, to get the black
man's ideal or to let his individuality work by its own gravity, as
it were. A conference of earnest Christian men have met at regular
intervals for some years past to discuss the best methods of promoting the welfare and development of colored people in this
country. Yet, strange as it may seem, they have never invited a
colored man or even intimated that one would be welcome to take
part in their deliberations. Their remedial contrivances are purely
theoretical or empirical, therefore, and the whole machinery devoid of soul.

The second important oversight in my judgment is closely allied
to this and probably grows out of it, and that is not developing
Negro womanhood as an essential fundamental for the elevation
of the race, and utilizing this agency in extending the work of
the Church.

Of the first I have possibly already presumed to say too much
since it does not strictly come within the province of my subject.
However, Macaulay somewhere criticises the Church of England
as not knowing how to use fanatics, and declares that had Ignatius
Loyola been in the Anglican instead of the Roman communion,

the Jesuits would have been schismatics instead of Catholics; and if the religious awakenings of the Wesleys had been in Rome, she would have shaven their heads, tied ropes around their waists and sent them out under her own banner and blessing.[11] Whether this be true or not, there is certainly a vast amount of force potential for Negro evangelization rendered latent, or worse, antagonistic by the halting, uncertain, I had almost said, trimming policy of the Church in the South. This may sound both presumptuous and ungrateful. It is mortifying, I know, to benevolent wisdom, after having spent itself in the execution of well conned theories for the ideal development of a particular work, to hear perhaps the weakest and humblest element of that work asking "what doest thou?"

Yet so it will be in life. The "thus far and no farther" pattern cannot be fitted to any growth in God's kingdom. The universal law of development is "onward and upward." It is God-given and inviolable. From the unfolding of the germ in the acorn to reach the sturdy oak, to the growth of a human soul into the full knowledge and likeness of its Creator, the breadth and scope of the movement in each and all are too grand, too mysterious, too like God himself, to be encompassed and locked down in human molds.

After all the Southern slave owners were right: either the very alphabet of intellectual growth must be forbidden and the Negro dealt with absolutely as a chattel having neither rights nor sensibilities; or else the clamps and irons of mental and moral, as well as civil compression must be riven asunder and the truly enfranchised soul led to the entrance of that boundless vista through which it is to toil upwards to its beckoning God as the buried seed germ to meet the sun.

A perpetual colored diaconate, carefully and kindly superintended by the white clergy; congregations of shiny faced peasants with their clean white aprons and sunbonnets catechised at regular

11. Saint Ignatius Loyola (1495–1556) was a Roman Catholic religious leader, founder of the Society of Jesus. Charles Wesley (1707–1788) and John Wesley (1703–1791) were clergymen of the Church of England and founders of Methodism.

intervals and taught to recite the creed, the Lord's prayer and the
ten commandments—duty towards God and duty towards neigh-
bor, surely such well tended sheep ought to be grateful to their
shepherds and content in that station of life to which it pleased
God to call them. True, like the old professor lecturing to his soli-
tary student, we make no provision here for irregularities. "Questions must be kept till after class," or dispensed with altogether.
That some do ask questions and insist on answers, in class too,
must be both impertinent and annoying. Let not our spiritual pas-
tors and masters however be grieved at such self-assertion as merely
signifies we have a destiny to fulfill and as men and women we
must be about our Father's business.

It is a mistake to suppose that the Negro is prejudiced against
a white ministry. Naturally there is not a more kindly and implicit
follower of a white man's guidance than the average colored peas-
ant. What would to others be an ordinary act of friendly or pas-
toral interest he would be more inclined to regard gratefully as a
condescension. And he never forgets such kindness. Could the
Negro be brought near to his white priest or bishop, he is not
suspicious. He is not only willing but often longs to unburden
his soul to this intelligent guide. There are no reservations when
he is convinced that you are his friend. It is a saddening satire on
American history and manners that it takes something to con-
vince him.

That our people are not "drawn" to a church whose chief dig-
nitaries they see only in the chancel, and whom they reverence as
they would a painting or an angel, whose life never comes down to
and touches theirs with the inspiration of an objective reality, may
be "perplexing" truly (American caste and American Christianity
both being facts) but it need not be surprising. There must be
something of human nature in it, the same as that which brought
about that "the Word was made flesh and dwelt among us" that
He might "draw" us towards God.

Men are not "drawn" by abstractions. Only sympathy and love
can draw, and until our Church in America realizes this and provides a clergy that can come in touch with our life and have a
fellow feeling for our woes, without being imbedded and frozen

up in their "Gothic antipathies," the good bishops are likely to continue "perplexed" by the sparsity of colored Episcopalians.

A colored priest of my acquaintance recently related to me, with tears in his eyes, how his reverend Father in God, the Bishop who had ordained him, had met him on the cars on his way to the diocesan convention and warned him, not unkindly, not to take a seat in the body of the convention with the white clergy. To avoid disturbance of their godly placidity he would of course please sit back and somewhat apart. I do not imagine that that clergyman had very much heart for the Christly (!) deliberations of that convention.

To return, however, it is not on this broader view of Church work, which I mentioned as a primary cause of its halting progress with the colored people, that I am to speak. My proper theme is the second oversight of which in my judgment our Christian propagandists have been guilty: or, the necessity of church training, protecting and uplifting our colored womanhood as indispensable to the evangelization of the race.

Apelles did not disdain even that criticism of his lofty art which came from an uncouth cobbler; and may I not hope that the writer's oneness with her subject both in feeling and in being may palliate undue obtrusiveness of opinions here.[12] That the race cannot be effectually lifted up till its women are truly elevated we take as proven. It is not for us to dwell on the needs, the neglects, and the ways of succor, pertaining to the black woman of the South. The ground has been ably discussed and an admirable and practical plan proposed by the oldest Negro priest in America, advising and urging that special organizations such as Church Sisterhoods and industrial schools be devised to meet her pressing needs in the Southland. That some such movements are vital to the life of this people and the extension of the Church among them, is not hard to see. Yet the pamphlet fell still-born from the press. So far as I am informed the Church has made no motion towards carrying out Dr. Crummell's suggestion.

The denomination which comes next our own in opposing

12. Apelles (fourth century B.C.) was a Greek artist.

the proverbial emotionalism of Negro worship in the South, and which in consequence like ours receives the cold shoulder from the old heads, resting as we do under the charge of not "having religion" and not believing in conversion—the Congregational-ists—have quietly gone to work on the young, have established industrial and training schools, and now almost every community in the South is yearly enriched by a fresh infusion of vigorous young hearts, cultivated heads, and helpful hands that have been trained at Fisk, at Hampton, in Atlanta University, and in Tuske-gee, Alabama.

These young people are missionaries actual or virtual both here and in Africa. They have learned to love the methods and doc-trines of the Church which trained and educated them; and so Congregationalism surely and steadily progresses.

Need I compare these well known facts with results shown by the Church in the same field and during the same or even a longer time.

The institution of the Church in the South to which she mainly looks for the training of her colored clergy and for the help of the "Black Woman" and "Colored Girl" of the South, has graduated since the year 1868, when the school was founded, five young women;[13] and while yearly numerous young men have been kept and trained for the ministry by the charities of the Church, the number of indigent females who have here been supported, shel-tered and trained, is phenomenally small. Indeed, to my mind, the attitude of the Church toward this feature of her work is as if the solution of the problem of Negro missions depended solely on sending a quota of deacons and priests into the field, girls being a sort of tertium quid whose development may be promoted if they can pay their way and fall in with the plans mapped out for the training of the other sex. Now I would ask in all earnest-ness, does not this force potential deserve by education and stimu-lus to be made dynamic? Is it not a solemn duty incumbent on all colored churchmen to make it so? Will not the aid of the Church be given to prepare our girls in head, heart, and hand for the duties

13. Cooper's note: "Five have been graduated since '86, two in '91, two in '92."

and responsibilities that await the intelligent wife, the Christian mother, the earnest, virtuous, helpful woman, at once both the lever and the fulcrum for uplifting the race.

As Negroes and churchmen we cannot be indifferent to these questions. They touch us most vitally on both sides. We believe in the Holy Catholic Church. We believe that however gigantic and apparently remote the consummation, the Church will go on conquering and to conquer till the kingdoms of this world, not excepting the black man and the black woman of the South, shall have become the kingdoms of the Lord and of his Christ.

That past work in this direction has been unsatisfactory we must admit. That without a change of policy results in the future will be as meagre, we greatly fear. Our life as a race is at stake. The dearest interests of our hearts are in the scales. We must either break away from dear old landmarks and plunge out in any line and every line that enables us to meet the pressing need of our people, or we must ask the Church to allow and help us, un-trammelled by the prejudices and theories of individuals, to work aggressively under her direction as we alone can, with God's help, for the salvation of our people.

The time is ripe for action. Self-seeking and ambition must be laid on the altar. The battle is one of sacrifice and hardship, but our duty is plain. We have been recipients of missionary bounty in some sort for twenty-one years. Not even the senseless vege-table is content to be a mere reservoir. Receiving without giving is an anomaly in nature. Nature's cells are all little workshops for manufacturing sunbeams, the product to be given out to earth's inhabitants in warmth, energy, thought, action. Inanimate cre-ation always pays back an equivalent.

Now, How much owest thou my Lord? Will his account be overdrawn if he call for singleness of purpose and self-sacrificing labor for your brethren? Having passed through your drill school, will you refuse a general's commission even if it entail responsi-bility, risk and anxiety, with possibly some adverse criticism? Is it too much to ask you to step forward and direct the work for your race along those lines which you know to be of first and vital importance?

Will you allow these words of Ralph Waldo Emerson? "In or-

dinary," says he, "we have a snappish criticism which watches
and contradicts the opposite party. We want the will which advances and dictates [acts]. Nature has made up her mind that what
cannot defend itself, shall not be defended. Complaining never so
loud and with never so much reason, is of no use. What cannot
stand must fall; and the measure of our sincerity and therefore of
the respect of men is the amount of health and wealth we will
hazard in the defense of our right."

5 IDA B. WELLS
(1862–1931)

Nothing is more definitely settled than he must act for himself. I have shown how he may employ the boycott, emigration and the press, and I feel that by a combination of all these agencies can be effectually stamped out lynch law, that last relic of barbarism and slavery. "The gods help those who help themselves."

—Ida B. Wells, "Southern Horrors"

IDA B. WELLS'S SPEECHES, MIRRORING HER LIFE, WERE BOLD, DIRECT, straightforward, and hard-hitting, yet honest and irrefutable. She, along with Frances Harper, Anna Cooper, and Fannie Williams, attended the 1893 World's Congress of Representative Women, part of the Columbian Exposition, in Chicago. But unlike her contemporaries, Wells had no official slot on the program of speakers. Instead, she positioned herself in front of the Haitian Pavilion, where Frederick Douglass was presiding, and distributed copies of an eighty-one page protest pamphlet with the telling title *The Reason Why the Colored American Is Not in the World's Columbian Exposition*. The pamphlet contained pieces written by Douglass; Ferdinand Barnett, a prominent Chicago attorney who later married Wells; I. Garland Penn, newspaperman; and Wells herself. Over ten thousand copies were circulated during the fair. But this issue was only one of many causes she espoused. In addition, Wells, the social activist, spoke out over a period of almost forty years, until her death in 1931, against the denial of women's rights and against racism generally, particularly against the practice of lynching. Not limiting herself to this country, she took her anti-lynching campaign to Europe and found favor there, even as she was being disparaged by the Southern press at home.

Wells was born a slave in Holly Springs, Mississippi, on July 16, 1862, the oldest of eight children. After emancipation, she enrolled in Shaw University (later renamed Rust College), which included all grade levels. In 1878, when Wells was sixteen, a yellow fever epidemic took the lives of her parents and her youngest brother. Wells insisted on keeping the family together and obtained a teaching job to support them. She eventually moved to Memphis, taking two of her sisters with her.

Her first years in Tennessee provided many opportunities to practice defiance. In May of 1884, when the conductor tried to remove her forcibly to the smoking car of a train, Wells resisted, and as she recalled it, "The moment he caught hold of my arm I fastened my teeth in the back of his hand" (Wells, *Crusade* 18). She brought a lawsuit against the railroad. Although she won the case, the railroad appealed and the decision was reversed in 1887. Yet the incident highlighted the rebellion and defiance characterizing Wells's lifelong struggle for personal and racial dignity.

Wells's insurgent spirit figured prominently in her teaching career. She joined a lyceum of schoolteachers and recited, discussed essays, and debated. She successfully edited the *Evening Star*, a small local paper, and began to write pieces for other black newspapers in the country. Seizing the opportunity to edit her own paper, she bought interest in the *Free Speech and Headlight* of Memphis in 1889. In one of her editorials, she protested the inferior conditions of the black schools and found herself without a teaching position the next term. She then devoted herself to journalism full time, soon becoming known as the "Princess of the Press." During this period of Wells's budding career as a journalist, events occurred that changed the direction of her life, which she describes vividly in the 1893 speech "Lynch Law in All Its Phases."

On October 5, 1892, she delivered her first speech at Lyric Hall in New York City at a testimonial that had been organized by a committee of 250 black women from New York and Brooklyn who were trying to raise money to help Wells reestablish the *Free Speech*.[1] The affair was considered by many "to be the greatest demonstration ever attempted by race women for one of their number" (Wells, *Crusade* 78). Of this first speaking experience Wells said, "Although every detail of that horrible lynching affair was imprinted in my memory, I had to commit it all to paper" (*Crusade* 79). The "horrible lynching affair" was the killing of three black Memphis entrepreneurs who opened a grocery store that was in competition with a white-owned establishment, which had a monopoly on the trade of the black population. The three black men were arrested for defending their store against white citizens who wanted to put them out of business. But before they had a chance to justify themselves, they were removed from their jail cells and murdered. Wells spoke out against this act in an editorial in her paper; as a result, the offices of the *Free Speech* were destroyed, and she was advised not to return to Memphis (she happened to be in Philadelphia visiting Frances Harper and attending a church conference when the editorial was published). Speaking of the testimonial, Wells says it was "the beginning of public speaking for me" (*Crusade* 81).

It was not until the next year, during a visit to Boston, that she first stood before a white audience. The address, delivered at Tremont Temple in the Boston Monday Lectureship on February 13, 1893, was "Lynch Law in All Its Phases." Wells had been invited to address the lectureship, formed in 1875 and comprised mainly of white clergymen and laymen and women who were prominent in Boston's intellectual life, by the organization's founder, Joseph Cook (Pointer 299).

Between the time of this speech and her "Southern Horrors" speech, one exceptionally gruesome lynching had occurred in Paris, Texas. She added this incident to her arsenal of evidence in the "Lynch Law" address. Other comparisons between the two speeches provide instructive contrast, as she adapted her material to a predominantly white audience further removed emotionally and geographically from the issues being addressed.

In both instances, Wells assumed the persona of investigative reporter, wanting the facts to speak for themselves. She was especially wary of emotional display. Delivering the Lyric Hall speech, she was annoyed that, when she described the murders of her three friends in Memphis, she began to cry. She commented: "Whatever my feelings, I am not given to public demonstrations. And only once before in all my life had I given way to woman's weakness in public" (*Crusade* 80). O'Connor, in *Pioneer Women Orators*, discusses the emphasis early women speakers placed on ethical rather than pathetic appeal. They wanted to establish an ethos of dignity for themselves as women who were "out of their sphere" in daring to speak publicly (159). Of course, this perception of impropriety would have been dimmer for Wells, speaking in the last decade of the nineteenth century, yet she was clearly concerned.[2]

Delivering "Lynch Law" a year later and to an audience no doubt less familiar with the particulars of the events, Wells described them in greater detail. Fully one-third of "Lynch Law" is a retelling of her previous three-year experience, from assuming editorship of the *Free Speech* to receiving warning that it would not be prudent to return to Memphis. She also gives a more careful accounting of her own changing perspective on this crisis, describing what for her and other prominent blacks was a "rude awakening" to the motives for lynching. Wells assumed here that her audience was simply uninformed, describing their indifference as "the result of ignorance of the true situation." She casts them in the role of "far-sighted Americans" who "desire to preserve our institutions," institutions clearly jeopardized by the practice of lynching.

As in her first speech, Wells's supporting examples come from the white press, in keeping with her claims that "out of their own mouths shall the murderers be condemned" ("Red Record" 15). She quotes from two white Memphis newspapers, *The Evening Scimitar* and the *Daily Commercial*, as well as from her own editorial in the *Free Speech*. Moving from the specific Memphis case, she argues for its typicality. Wells cites statistics covering the past ten years, and analyzes the Italian lynching of 1891. She apologetically details two more recent lynching episodes, including how in the burning of Henry Smith of Paris, Texas, "hot irons were run down his throat and cooked his tongue."

Perhaps her most compelling analogy in "Lynch Law" is the one she draws between the horrors of lynching and the horrors of slavery. As with slavery, she argues, a horrible situation exists in one part of the country that the citizens of another part refuse to believe, are unaware of, or choose not to address. "The lawlessness," says Wells, "which has been here described is like unto that which prevailed under slavery."

The speech ends with a different proposal for action than that of the Lyric Hall address, in which she asks her African-American audience to boycott, emigrate, and engage in investigative reporting. From her Boston audience, she asks for a general outcry against the atrocities. The final, practical appeal in "Lynch Law" is in keeping with Wells's insistence that the facts themselves must make the case: do not act out of pity or even out of a sense of justice but out of the desire to preserve democracy.

NOTE

1. The speech, "Southern Horrors: Lynch Law in All Its Phases" (1892), can be found in Ida B. Wells-Barnett, *On Lynchings: Southern Horror, A Red Record, Mob Rule in New Orleans* (reprint, Salem, NH: Ayer, 1990), 4–24. One of the organizers of the testimonial was Victoria Matthews, whose speech "The Value of Race Literature " can be found in this collection.

2. For analysis of rhetorical strategies in this speech, see Shirley W. Logan, "Rhetorical Strategies in Ida B. Wells's 'Southern Horrors: Lynch Law in All Its Phases.'" *SAGE: A Scholarly Journal on Black Women* 8 (Summer 1991): 3–9.

LYNCH LAW IN ALL ITS PHASES
(1893)

I AM BEFORE THE AMERICAN PEOPLE TO-DAY THROUGH NO INCLINA-
tion of my own, but because of a deep-seated conviction that the
country at large does not know the extent to which lynch law
prevails in parts of the Republic, nor the conditions which force
into exile those who speak the truth. I cannot believe that the apa-
thy and indifference which so largely obtains regarding mob rule
is other than the result of ignorance of the true situation. And
yet, the observing and thoughtful must know that in one section,
at least, of our common country, a government of the people, by
the people, and for the people, means a government by the mob;
where the land of the free and home of the brave means a land
of lawlessness, murder and outrage; and where liberty of speech
means the license of might to destroy the business and drive from
home those who exercise this privilege contrary to the will of the
mob. Repeated attacks on the life, liberty and happiness of any
citizen or class of citizens are attacks on distinctive American institutions; such attacks imperiling as they do the foundation of
government, law and order, merit the thoughtful consideration
of far-sighted Americans; not from a standpoint of sentiment, not
even so much from a standpoint of justice to a weak race, as from
a desire to preserve our institutions.

The race problem or negro question, as it has been called, has
been omnipresent and all-pervading since long before the Afro-
American was raised from the degradation of the slave to the dignity of the citizen. It has never been settled because the right methods have not been employed in the solution. It is the Banquo's
ghost of politics, religion, and sociology which will not down at
the bidding of those who are tormented with its ubiquitous appearance on every occasion. Times without number, since invested with citizenship, the race has been indicted for ignorance,
immorality and general worthlessness—declared guilty and executed by its self-constituted judges. The operations of law do not
dispose of negroes fast enough, and lynching bees have become
the favorite pastime of the South. As excuse for the same, a new
cry, as false as it is foul, is raised in an effort to blast race character,

a cry which has proclaimed to the world that virtue and innocence are violated by Afro-Americans who must be killed like wild beasts to protect womanhood and childhood.

Born and reared in the South, I had never expected to live elsewhere. Until this past year I was one among those who believed the condition of the masses gave large excuse for the humiliations and proscriptions under which we labored; that when wealth, education and character became more general among us, the cause being removed the effect would cease, and justice be accorded to all alike. I shared the general belief that good newspapers entering regularly the homes of our people in every state could do more to bring about this result than any agency. Preaching the doctrine of self-help, thrift and economy every week, they would be the teachers to those who had been deprived of school advantages, yet were making history every day—and train to think for themselves our mental children of a larger growth. And so, three years ago last June, I became editor and part owner of the *Memphis Free Speech*. As editor, I had occasion to criticize the city School Board's employment of inefficient teachers and poor school-buildings for Afro-American children. I was in the employ of that board at the time, and at the close of that school-term one year ago, was not re-elected to a position I had held in the city schools for seven years. Accepting the decision of the Board of Education, I set out to make a race newspaper pay—a thing which older and wiser heads said could not be done. But there were enough of our people in Memphis and surrounding territory to support a paper, and I believed they would do so. With nine months hard work the circulation increased from 1,500 to 3,500; in twelve months it was on a good paying basis. Throughout the Mississippi Valley in Arkansas, Tennessee and Mississippi on plantations and in towns, the demand for and interest in the paper increased among the masses. The newsboys who would not sell it on the trains, voluntarily testified that they had never known colored people to demand a paper so eagerly.

To make the paper a paying business I became advertising agent, solicitor, as well as editor, and was continually on the go. Wherever I went among the people, I gave them in church, school, public gatherings, and home, the benefit of my honest conviction that maintenance of character, money getting and education would finally solve our problem and that it depended on us to say how soon this would be brought about. This sentiment bore good fruit in Memphis. We had nice homes, representatives in almost every branch of business and profession, and refined society. We had learned that helping each other helped all, and every well-conducted business by Afro-Americans prospered. With all our proscription in theatres, hotels and on railroads, we had never had a lynching and did not believe we could have one. There had been lynchings and brutal outrages of all sorts in our own state and those adjoining us, but we had confidence and pride in our city and the majesty of its laws. So far in advance of other Southern cities was ours, we were content to endure the evils we had, to labor and to wait.

But there was a rude awakening. On the morning of March 9, the bodies of three of our best young men were found in an old field horribly shot to pieces. These young men had owned and operated the "People's Grocery," situated at what was known as the Curve—a suburb made up almost entirely of colored people—about a mile from city limits. Thomas Moss, one of the oldest letter-carriers in the city, was president of the company, Calvin McDowell was manager and Will Stewart was a clerk. There were about ten other stockholders, all colored men. The young men were well known and popular and their business flourished, and that of Barrett, a white grocer who kept store there before the "People's Grocery" was established, went down. One day an officer came to the "People's Grocery" and inquired for a colored man who lived in the neighborhood, and for whom the officer had a warrant. Barrett was with him and when McDowell said he knew nothing as to the whereabouts of the man for whom they were searching, Barrett, not the officer, then accused McDowell of harboring the man, and McDowell gave the lie. Barrett drew his pistol and struck McDowell with it; thereupon McDowell, who was a tall, fine-looking six-footer, took Barrett's pistol from him, knocked him down and gave him a good thrashing, while Will Stewart, the clerk, kept the special officer at bay. Barrett went to town, swore out a warrant for their arrest on a charge of assault and battery. McDowell went before the Criminal Court, immediately gave bond and returned to his store. Barrett then threatened (to use his own words) that he was going to clean out the whole store. Knowing how anxious he was to destroy their business, these young men consulted a lawyer who told them they were justified in defending themselves if attacked, as they were a mile beyond city limits and police protection. They accordingly armed several of their friends not to assail, but to resist the threatened Saturday night attack.

When they saw Barrett enter the front door and a half dozen men at the rear door at 11 o'clock that night, they supposed the attack was on and immediately fired into the crowd, wounding three men. These men, dressed in citizen's clothes, turned out to be deputies who claimed to be hunting another man for whom they had a warrant, and whom any one of them could have arrested without trouble. When these men found they had fired upon officers of the law, they threw away their firearms and submitted to arrest, confident they should establish their innocence of intent to fire upon officers of the law. The daily papers in flaming headlines roused the evil passions of the whites, denounced these poor boys in unmeasured terms, nor permitted them a word in their own defense.

The neighborhood of the Curve was searched next day, and about thirty persons were thrown into jail, charged with conspiracy. No communication was to be had with friends any of the three days these men were in jail; bail was refused and Thomas Moss was not allowed to eat the food his wife prepared for him. The judge is reported to have said, "Any one can see them after three days." They were seen after three days, but they were no longer able to respond to the greetings of friends. On Tuesday following the shooting at the grocery, the papers which had made much of the sufferings of the wounded deputies, and promised it would go hard with those who did the shooting, if they died, announced that the officers were all out of danger, and would recover. The friends of the prisoners breathed more easily and relaxed their vigilance. They felt that as the officers would not die, there was no danger that in the heat of passion the prisoners would meet violent death at the hands of the mob. Besides, we had such confidence in the law. But the law did not provide capital punishment for shooting which did not kill. So the mob did what the law could not be made to do, as a lesson to the Afro-American that he must not shoot a white man, no matter what the provocation. The same night after the announcement was made in the papers that the officers would get well, the mob, in obedience to a plan known to every prominent white man in the city, went to the jail between two and three o'clock in the morning, dragged out these young men, hatless and shoeless, put them on the yard engine of the railroad which was in waiting just behind the jail, carried them a mile north of city limits and horribly shot them to death while the locomotive at a given signal let off steam and blew the whistle to deaden the sound of the firing.

"It was done by unknown men," said the jury, yet the *Appeal-Avalanche*, which goes to press at 3 a.m., had a two-column account of the lynching. The papers also told how McDowell got hold of the guns of the mob, and as his grasp could not be loosened, his hand was shattered with a pistol ball and all the lower part of his face was torn away. There were four pools of blood found and only three bodies. It was whispered that he, McDowell, killed one of the lynchers with his gun, and it is well known that a policeman who was seen on the street a few days previous to the lynching, died very suddenly the next day after.

"It was done by unknown parties," said the jury, yet the papers told how Tom Moss begged for his life, for the sake of his wife, his little daughter and his unborn infant. They also told us that his last words were, "If you will kill us, turn our faces to the West."

All this we learned too late to save these men, even if the law had not been in the hands of their murderers. When the colored people realized that the flower of our young manhood had been stolen away at night and murdered, there was a rush for firearms to avenge the wrong, but no house would sell a colored man a gun; the armory of the Tennessee Rifles, our only colored military company, and of which McDowell was a member, was broken into by order of the Criminal Court judge, and its guns taken. One hundred men and irresponsible boys from fifteen years and up were armed by order of the authorities and rushed out to the Curve, where it was reported that the colored people were mass-ing, and at point of the bayonet dispersed these men who could do nothing but talk. The cigars, wines, etc., of the grocery stock were freely used by the mob, who possessed the place on pretence of dispersing the conspiracy. The money drawer was broken into and contents taken. The trunk of Calvin McDowell, who had a room in the store, was broken open, and his clothing, which was not good enough to take away, was thrown out and trampled on the floor.

These men were murdered, their stock was attached by creditors and sold for less than one-eighth of its cost to that same man Barrett, who is to-day running his grocery in the same place. He had indeed kept his word, and by aid of the authorities destroyed the People's Grocery Company root and branch. The relatives of Will Stewart and Calvin McDowell are bereft of their protectors. The baby daughter of Tom Moss, too young to express how she misses her father, toddles to the wardrobe, seizes the legs of the trousers of his letter-carrier uniform, hugs and kisses them with evident delight and stretches up her little hands to be taken up into the arms which will nevermore clasp his daughter's form. His wife holds Thomas Moss, Jr., in her arms, upon whose unconscious baby face the tears fall thick and fast when she is thinking of the sad fate of the father he will never see, and of the two helpless children who cling to her for the support she cannot give. Although these men were peaceable, law-abiding citizens of this country, we are told there can be no punishment for their murderers nor indemnity for their relatives.

I have no power to describe the feeling of horror that possessed every member of the race in Memphis when the truth dawned upon us that the protection of the law which we had so long enjoyed was no longer ours; all this had been destroyed in a night, and the barriers of the law had been thrown down, and the guardians of the public peace and confidence scoffed away into the shadows, and all authority given into the hands of the mob, and innocent men cut down as if they were brutes—the first feeling was one of utter dismay, then intense indignation. Vengeance was whispered from ear to ear, but sober reflection brought the conviction that it would be extreme folly to seek vengeance when such action meant certain death for the men, and horrible slaughter for the women and children, as one of the evening papers took care to remind us. The power of the State, country and city, the civil authorities and the strong arm of the military power were all on the side of the mob and of lawlessness. Few of our men possessed firearms, our only company's guns were confiscated, and the only white man who would sell a colored man a gun, was himself jailed, and his store closed. We were helpless in our great strength. It was our first object lesson in the doctrine of white supremacy; an illustration of the South's cardinal principle that no matter what the attainments, character or standing of an Afro-American, the laws of the South will not protect him against a white man.

There was only one thing we could do, and a great determination seized upon the people to follow the advice of the martyred Moss, and "turn our faces to the West," whose laws protect all alike. The *Free Speech* supported by our ministers and leading business men advised the people to leave a community whose laws did not protect them. Hundreds left on foot to walk four hundred miles between Memphis and Oklahoma. A Baptist minister went to the territory, built a church, and took his entire congregation out in less than a month. Another minister sold his church and took his flock to California, and still another has settled in Kansas. In two months, six thousand persons had left the city and every branch of business began to feel this silent resentment of the outrage, and failure of the authorities to punish the lynchers. There were a number of business failures and blocks of houses were for rent. The superintendent and treasurer of the street railway company called at the office of the *Free Speech*, to have us urge the colored people to ride again on the street cars. A real estate dealer said to a colored man who returned some property he had been buying on the installment plan: "I don't see what you 'niggers' are cutting up about. You got off light. We first intended to kill every one of those thirty-one 'niggers' in jail, but concluded to let all go but the 'leaders.'" They did let all go to the penitentiary. These so-called rioters have since been tried in the Criminal Court for the conspiracy of defending their property, and are now serving terms of three, eight, and fifteen years each in the Tennessee State prison.

To restore the equilibrium and put a stop to the great financial loss, the next move was to get rid of the *Free Speech*, the disturbing element which kept the waters troubled; which would not let the people forget, and in obedience to whose advice nearly six thousand persons had left the city. In casting about for an excuse, the mob found it in the following editorial which appeared in the Memphis *Free Speech*, May 21, 1892:

> Eight negroes lynched in one week. Since last issue of the *Free Speech* one was lynched at Little Rock, Ark., where the citizens broke into the penitentiary and got their man; three near Anniston, Ala., and one in New Orleans, all on the same charge, the new alarm of assaulting white women and three near Clarksville, Ga., for killing a white man. The same program of hanging then shooting bullets into the lifeless bodies was carried out to the letter. Nobody in this section of the country believes the old threadbare lie that negro men rape white women. If Southern white men are not careful they will overreach themselves, and public sentiment will have a reaction. A conclusion will then be reached which will be very damaging to the moral reputation of their women.

Commenting on this, *The Daily Commercial* of Wednesday following said:

> Those negroes who are attempting to make lynching of individuals of their race a means for arousing the worst passions of their kind, are playing with a dangerous sentiment. The negroes may as well understand that there is no mercy for the negro rapist, and little patience with his defenders. A negro organ printed in this city in a recent issue published the following atrocious paragraph: "Nobody in this section believes the old threadbare lie that negro men rape white women. If Southern white men are not careful they will overreach themselves and public sentiment will have a reaction. A conclusion will be reached which will be very damaging to the moral reputation of

their women." The fact that a black scoundrel is allowed
to live and utter such loathsome and repulsive calumnies
is a volume of evidence as to the wonderful patience of
Southern whites. There are some things the Southern
white man will not tolerate, and the obscene intimidation
of the foregoing has brought the writer to the very utter-
most limit of public patience. We hope we have said
enough.

The *Evening Scimitar* of the same day copied this leading editorial and added this comment: "Patience under such circumstances
is not a virtue. If the negroes themselves do not apply the remedy
without delay, it will be the duty of those he has attacked, to tie
the wretch who utters these calumnies to a stake at the intersection
of Main and Madison streets, brand him in the forehead with a
hot iron and—"

Such open suggestions by the leading daily papers of the progressive city of Memphis were acted upon by the leading citizens
and a meeting was held at the Cotton Exchange that evening. *The
Commercial* two days later had the following account of it:

Atrocious Blackguardism.
There will be no Lynching and no Repetition of the Offense.

In its issue of Wednesday *The Commercial* reproduced and
commented upon an editorial which appeared a day or
two before in a negro organ known as the *Free Speech.*
The article was so insufferably and indecently slanderous
that the whole city awoke to a feeling of intense resentment which came within an ace of culminating in one of
those occurrences whose details are so eagerly seized and
so prominently published by Northern newspapers. Con-
servative counsels, however, prevailed, and no extreme
measures were resorted to. On Wednesday afternoon a
meeting of citizens was held. It was not an assemblage of
hoodlums or irresponsible fire-eaters, but solid, substan-
tial business men who knew exactly what they were

doing and who were far more indignant at the villainous
insult to the women of the South than they would have
been at any injury done themselves. This meeting appointed a committee to seek the author of the infamous
editorial and warn him quietly that upon repetition of the
offense he would find some other part of the country a
good deal safer and pleasanter place of residence than this.
The committee called a negro preacher named Nightingale, but he disclaimed responsibility and convinced the
gentlemen that he had really sold out his paper to a
woman named Wells. This woman is not in Memphis at
present. It was finally learned that one Fleming, a negro
who was driven out of Crittenden Co. during the trouble
there a few years ago, wrote the paragraph. He had, however, heard of the meeting, and fled from a fate which he
feared was in store for him, and which he knew he deserved. His whereabouts could not be ascertained, and the
committee so reported. Later on, a communication from
Fleming to a prominent Republican politician, and that
politician's reply were shown to one or two gentlemen.
The former was an inquiry as to whether the writer
might safely return to Memphis, the latter was an em-
phatic answer in the negative, and Fleming is still in hid-
ing. Nothing further will be done in the matter. There
will be no lynching, and it is very certain there will be
no repetition of the outrage. If there should be Friday,
May 25.

The only reason there was no lynching of Mr. Fleming who was
business manager and half owner of the *Free Speech*, and who did
not write the editorial, was because this same white Republican
told him the committee was coming, and warned him not to trust
them, but get out of the way. The committee scoured the city
hunting him, and had to be content with Mr. Nightingale who
was dragged to the meeting, shamefully abused (although it was
known he had sold out his interest in the paper six months before).
He was struck in the face and forced at the pistol's point to sign

a letter which was written by them, in which he denied all knowledge of the editorial, denounced and condemned it as slander on white women. I do not censure Mr. Nightingale for his action because, having never been at the pistol's point myself, I do not feel that I am competent to sit in judgment on him, or say what I would do under such circumstances.

I had written that editorial with other matter for the week's paper before leaving home the Friday previous for the General Conference of the A.M.E. Church in Philadelphia. Conference adjourned Tuesday, and Thursday, May 25, at 3 p.m., I landed in New York City for a few days' stay before returning home, and there learned from the papers that my business manager had been driven away and the paper suspended. Telegraphing for news, I received telegrams and letters in return informing me that the trains were being watched, that I was to be dumped into the river and beaten, if not killed; it had been learned that I wrote the editorial and I was to be hanged in front of the court-house and my face bled if I returned, and I was implored by my friends to remain away. The creditors attached the office in the meantime and the outfit was sold without more ado, thus destroying effectually that which it had taken years to build. One prominent insurance agent publicly declares he will make it his business to shoot me down on sight if I return to Memphis in twenty years, while a leading white lady had remarked that she was opposed to the lynching of those three men in March, but she did wish there was some way by which I could be gotten back and lynched.

I have been censured for writing that editorial, but when I think of the five men who were lynched that week for assault on white women and that not a week passes but some poor soul is violently ushered into eternity on this trumped-up charge, knowing the many things I do, and part of which I tried to tell in the *New York Age* of June 25, (and in the pamphlets I have with me)[1] seeing that the whole race in the South was injured in the estimation of the world because of these false reports, I could no longer hold my

1. Wells used the testimonial gift from the 1892 fundraiser held for her in New York City to publish the pamphlet *Southern Horrors*, relating her experiences in Memphis.

peace, and I feel, yes, I am sure, that if it had to be done over again (provided no one else was the loser save myself) I would do and say the very same again.

The lawlessness here described is not confined to one locality. In the past ten years over a thousand colored men, women and children have been butchered, murdered and burnt in all parts of the South. The details of these horrible outrages seldom reach beyond the narrow world where they occur. Those who commit the murders write the reports, and hence these lasting blots upon the honor of a nation cause but a faint ripple on the outside world. They arouse no great indignation and call forth no adequate demand for justice. The victims were black, and the reports are so written as to make it appear that the helpless creatures deserved the fate which overtook them.

Not so with the Italian lynching of 1891. They were not black men, and three of them were not citizens of the Republic, but subjects of the King of Italy. The chief of police of New Orleans was shot and eleven Italians were arrested charged with the murder; they were tried and the jury disagreed; the good, law-abiding citizens of New Orleans thereupon took them from the jail and lynched them at high noon. A feeling of horror ran through the nation at this outrage. All Europe was amazed. The Italian government demanded thorough investigation and redress, and the Federal Government promised to give the matter the consideration which was its due. The diplomatic relations between the two countries became very much strained and for a while war talk was freely indulged. Here was a case where the power of the Federal Government to protect its own citizens and redeem its pledges to a friendly power was put to the test. When our State Department called upon the authorities of Louisiana for investigation of the crime and punishment of the criminals, the United States government was told that the crime was strictly within the authority of the State of Louisiana, and Louisiana would attend to it. After a farcical investigation, the usual verdict in such cases was rendered: "Death at the hand of parties unknown to the jury," the same verdict which has been pronounced over the bodies of over 1,000 colored persons! Our general government has thus admitted that it has no jurisdiction over the crimes committed at

New Orleans upon citizens of the country, nor upon those citizens of a friendly power to whom the general government and not the State government has pledged protection. Not only has our general government made the confession that one of the states is greater than the Union, but the general government has paid $25,000 of the people's money to the King of Italy for the lynching of those three subjects, the evil-doing of one State, over which it has no control, but for whose lawlessness the whole country must pay. The principle involved in the treaty power of the government has not yet been settled to the satisfaction of foreign powers; but the principle involved in the right of State jurisdiction in such matters, was settled long ago by the decision of the United States Supreme Court.

I beg your patience while we look at another phase of the lynching mania. We have turned heretofore to the pages of ancient and medieval history, to Roman tyranny, the Jesuitical Inquisition of Spain for the spectacle of a human being burnt to death. In the past ten years three instances, at least, have been furnished where men have literally been roasted to death to appease the fury of Southern mobs. The Texarkana instance of last year and the Paris, Texas, case of this month are the most recent as they are the most shocking and repulsive. Both were charged with crimes from which the laws provide adequate punishment. The Texarkana man, Ed Coy, was charge with assaulting a white woman. A mob pronounced him guilty, strapped him to a tree, chipped the flesh from his body, poured coal oil over him and the woman in the case set fire to him. The country looked on and in many cases applauded, because it was published that this man had violated the honor of the white woman, although he protested his innocence to the last. Judge Tourgee in the Chicago *Inter Ocean* of recent date says investigation has shown that Ed Coy had supported this woman, (who was known to be of bad character,) and her drunken husband for over a year previous to the burning.

The Paris, Texas, burning of Henry Smith, February 1st, has exceeded all the others in its horrible details. The man was drawn through the streets on a float, as the Roman generals used to parade their trophies of war, while the scaffold ten feet high, was being built, and irons were heated in the fire. He was bound on it, and red-hot irons began at his feet and slowly branded his body, while the mob howled with delight at his shrieks. Red hot irons were run down his throat and cooked his tongue; his eyes were burned out, and when he was at last unconscious, cotton seed hulls were placed under him, coal oil poured all over him, and a torch applied to the mass. When the flames burned away the ropes which bound Smith and scorched his flesh, he was brought back to sensibility and burned and maimed and sightless as he was, he rolled off the platform and away from the fire. His half-cooked body was seized and trampled and thrown back into the flames while a mob of twenty thousand persons who came from all over the country howled with delight, and gathered up some buttons and ashes after all was over to preserve for relics. This man was charged with outraging and murdering a four-year-old white child, covering her body with brush, sleeping beside her through the night, then making his escape. If true, it was the deed of a mad-man, and should have been clearly proven so. The fact that no time for verification of the newspaper reports was given, is suspicious, especially when I remember that a negro was lynched in Indianola, Sharkey Co., Miss., last summer. The dispatches said it was because he had assaulted the sheriff's eight-year-old daughter. The girl was more than eighteen years old and was found by her father in this man's room, who was a servant on the place.

These incidents have been made the basis of this terrible story because they overshadow all others of a like nature in cruelty and represent the legal phases of the whole question. They could be multiplied without number and each outrival the other in the fiendish cruelty exercised, and the frequent awful lawlessness exhibited. The following table shows the number of black men lynched from January 1, 1882, to January 1, 1892: In 1882, 52; 1883, 39; 1884, 53; 1885, 77; 1886, 73; 1887, 70; 1888, 72; 1889, 95; 1890, 100; 1891, 169. Of these 728 [*sic* 800] black men who were murdered, 269 were charged with rape, 253 with murder, 44 with robbery, 37 with incendiarism, 32 with reasons unstated (it was not necessary to have a reason), 27 with race prejudice, 13 with quarreling with white men, 10 with making threats, 7 with rioting, 5 with miscegenation, 4 with burglary. One of the men lynched in 1891 was Will Lewis, who was lynched because "he was

drunk and saucy to white folks." A woman who was one of the
73 victims in 1886, was hung in Jackson, Tenn., because the white
woman for whom she cooked, died suddenly of poisoning. An
examination showed arsenical poisoning. A search in the cook's
room found rat poison. She was thrown into jail, and when the
mob had worked itself up to the lynching pitch, she was dragged
out, every stitch of clothing torn from her body, and was hung
in the public court house square in sight of everybody. That white
woman's husband has since died, in the insane asylum, a raving
maniac, and his ravings have led to the conclusion that he and not
the cook, was the poisoner of his wife. A fifteen-year-old colored
girl was lynched last spring, at Rayville, La., on the same charge
of poisoning. A woman was also lynched at Hollendale, Miss.,
last spring, charged with being an accomplice in the murder of
her white paramour who had abused her. These were only two
of the 159 persons lynched in the South from January 1, 1892,
to January 1, 1893. Over a dozen black men have been lynched
already since this new year set in, and the year is not yet two
months old.

It will thus be seen that neither age, sex nor decency are spared.
Although the impression has gone abroad that most of the lynchings take place because of assaults on white women only one-third
of the number lynched in the past ten years have been charged
with that offense, to say nothing of those who were not guilty of
the charge. And according to law none of them were guilty until
proven so. But the unsupported word of any white person for
any cause is sufficient to cause a lynching. So bold have the lynchers become, masks are laid aside, the temples of justice and strong-
holds of law are invaded in broad daylight and prisoners taken out
and lynched, while governors of states and officers of law stand
by and see the work well done.

And yet this Christian nation, the flower of the nineteenth
century civilization, says it can do nothing to stop this inhuman
slaughter. The general government is willingly powerless to send
troops to protect the lives of its black citizens, but the state gov-
ernments are free to use state troops to shoot them down like
cattle, when in desperation the black men attempt to defend themselves, and then tell the world that it was necessary to put down
a "race war."

Persons unfamiliar with the condition of affairs in the Southern States do not credit the truth when it is told them. They cannot conceive how such a condition of affairs prevails so near them with steam power, telegraph wires and printing presses in daily and hourly touch with the localities where such disorder reigns. In a former generation the ancestors of these same people refused to believe that slavery was the "league with death and the covenant with hell." Wm. Lloyd Garrison declared it to be, until he was thrown into a dungeon in Baltimore, until the signal lights of Nat Turner lit the dull skies of Northampton County, and until sturdy old John Brown made his attack on Harper's Ferry. When freedom of speech was martyred in the person of Elijah Lovejoy at Alton, when the liberty of free-discussion in Senate of the Nation's Congress was struck down in the person of the fearless Charles Sumner, the Nation was at last convinced that slavery was not only a monster but a tyrant.[2] That same tyrant is at work under a new name and guise. The lawlessness which has been here described is like unto that which prevailed under slavery. *The very same forces are at work now as then.* The attempt is being made to subject to a condition of civil and industrial dependence, those whom the Constitution declares to be free men. The events which have led up to the present wide-spread lawlessness in the South can be traced to the very first year Lee's conquered veterans marched from Appomattox to their homes in the Southland. They were conquered in war, but not in spirit. They believed as firmly as ever that it was their right to rule black men and dictate to the National Government. The Knights of White Liners, and the Ku Klux Klans were composed of veterans of the Confederate army who were determined to destroy the effect of all the slave had gained by the war. They finally accomplished their purpose in 1876. The right of the Afro-American to vote and hold office remains in the Federal Constitution, but is destroyed in the constitution of the Southern states. Having destroyed the citizenship

2. Elijah Lovejoy (1802–1837) was a clergyman and editor of a religious newspaper. He was killed by an angry mob trying to stop the publication of his abolitionist editorials in the *Alton* (Illinois) *Observer*. Charles Sumner (1811–1874) was an American statesman and antislavery leader who died fighting for a civil rights bill to ban discrimination and segregation in public facilities.

of the man, they are now trying to destroy the manhood of the citizen. All their laws are shaped to this end, school laws, railroad car regulations, those governing labor liens on crops, every device is adopted to make slaves of free men and rob them of their wages. Whenever a malicious law is violated in any of its parts, any farmer, any railroad conductor, or merchant can call together a posse of his neighbors and punish even with death the black man who resists and the legal authorities sanction what is done by failing to prosecute and punish the murderers. The Repeal of the Civil Rights Law removed their last barrier and the black man's last bulwark and refuge.[3] The rule of the mob is absolute.

Those who know this recital to be true, say there is nothing they can do—they cannot interfere and vainly hope by further concession to placate the imperious and dominating part of our country in which this lawlessness prevails. Because this country has been almost rent in twain by internal dissension, the other sections seem virtually to have agreed that the best way to heal the breach is to permit the taking away of civil, political, and even human rights, to stand by in silence and utter indifference while the South continues to wreak fiendish vengeance on the irresponsible cause. They pretend to believe that with all the machinery of law and government in its hands; with the jails and penitentiaries and convict farms filled with petty race criminals; with the well-known fact that no negro has ever been known to escape conviction and punishment for any crime in the South—still there are those who try to justify and condone the lynching of over a thousand black men in less than ten years—an average of one hundred a year. The public sentiment of the country, by its silence in press, pulpit and in public meetings has encouraged this state of affairs, and public sentiment is stronger than law. With all the country's disposition to condone and temporize with the South and its methods; with its many instances of sacrificing principle to prejudice for the sake of making friends and healing the breach made by the late war; of going into the lawless country with capi-

3. In 1883, the U.S. Supreme Court declared the Civil Rights Act of 1875, granting the right to equal treatment for African-Americans in public entertainment facilities, unconstitutional.

tal to build up its waste places and remaining silent in the presence of outrage and wrong the South is as vindictive and bitter as ever. She is willing to make friends as long as she is permitted to pursue unmolested and uncensured, her course of proscription, injustice, outrage and vituperation. The malignant misrepresentation of General Butler, the uniformly indecent and abusive assault of this dead man whose only crime was a defence of his country, is a recent proof that the South has lost none of its bitterness.[4] The *Nashville American*, one of the leading papers of one of the leading southern cities, gleefully announced editorially that " 'The Beast is dead.' Early yesterday morning, acting under the devil's orders, the angel of Death took Ben Butler and landed him in the lowest depths of hell, and we pity even the devil the possession he has secured." The men who wrote these editorials are without exception young men who know nothing of slavery and scarcely anything of the war. The bitterness and hatred have been instilled in and taught them by their parents, and they are men who make and reflect the sentiment of their section. The South spares nobody else's feelings, and it seems a queer logic that when it comes to a question of right, involving lives of citizens and the honor of the government, the South's feelings must be respected and spared.

Do you ask the remedy? A public sentiment strong against lawlessness must be aroused. Every individual can contribute to this awakening. When a sentiment against lynch law as strong, deep and mighty as that roused against slavery prevails, I have no fear of the result. It should be already established as a fact and not as a theory, that every human being must have a fair trial for his life and liberty, no matter what the charge against him. When a demand goes up from fearless and persistent reformers from press and pulpit, from industrial and moral associations that this shall be so from Maine to Texas and from ocean to ocean, a way will be found to make it so.

In deference to the few words of condemnation uttered at the M.E. [Methodist Episcopal] General Conference last year, and

---

4. Benjamin Franklin Butler (1818–1893) was a general in the Union army.

by other organizations, Governors Hogg of Texas, Northern of
Georgia, and Tillman of South Carolina, have issued proclama-
tions offering rewards for the apprehension of lynchers. These
rewards have never been claimed, and these governors knew they
would not be when offered. In many cases they knew the ring-
leaders of the mobs. The prosecuting attorney of Shelby County,
Tenn., wrote Governor Buchanan to offer a reward for the arrest of the lynchers of three young men murdered in Memphis.
Everybody in that city and state knew well that the letter was
written for the sake of effect and the governor did not even offer
the reward. But the country at large deluded itself with the belief
that the officials of the South and the leading citizens condemned
lynching. The lynchings go on in spite of offered rewards, and in
face of Governor Hogg's vigorous talk, the second man was burnt
alive in his state with the utmost deliberation and publicity. Since
he sent a message to the legislature the mob found and hung Henry
Smith's stepson, because he refused to tell where Smith was when
they were hunting for him. Public sentiment which shall denounce
these crimes in season and out; public sentiment which turns capital and immigration from a section given over to lawlessness; public sentiment which insists on the punishment of criminals and
lynchers by law must be aroused.

It is no wonder in my mind that the party which stood for
thirty years as the champion of human liberty and human rights,
the party of great moral ideas, should suffer overwhelming defeat
when it has proven recreant to its professions and abandoned a
position it created; when although its followers were being out-
raged in every sense, it was afraid to stand for the right, and appeal
to the American people to sustain them in it. It put aside the question of a free ballot and fair count of every citizen and gave its
voice and influence for the protection of the coat instead of the
man who wore it, for the product of labor instead of the laborer;
for the seal of citizenship rather than the citizen, and insisted upon
the evils of free trade instead of the sacredness of free speech. I
am no politician but I believe if the Republican party had met the
issues squarely for human rights instead of the tariff it would have
occupied a different position to-day. The voice of the people is
the voice of God, and I long with all the intensity of my soul for

the Garrison, Douglas[s], Sumner, W[h]ittier and Phillips who shall rouse this nation to a demand that from Greenland's icy mountains to the coral reefs of the Southern seas, mob rule shall be put down and equal and exact justice be accorded to every citizen of whatever race, who finds a home within the borders of the land of the free and the home of the brave.[5]

Then no longer will our national hymn be sounding brass and a tinkling cymbal, but every member of this great composite nation will be a living, harmonious illustration of the words, and all can honestly and gladly join in singing:

My country! 'tis of thee, Sweet land of liberty
Of thee I sing.
Land where our fathers died,
Land of the Pilgrim's pride,
From every mountain side
Freedom does ring.

5. John Greenleaf Whittier (1807–1892) was an American poet known as the poet of abolition for his attacks against slavery. Wendell Phillips (1811–1884), "abolition's golden trumpet," was uncompromising in his opposition to slavery.

6 FANNIE BARRIER WILLIAMS
(1855–1944)

> She is the only woman in America who is almost un-
> known; the only woman for whom nothing is done; the
> only woman without sufficient defenders when assailed;
> the only woman who is still outside of that world of chiv-
> alry that in all the ages has apotheosized woman kind. . . .
> Yet colored women must face an age in this part of the
> world, that insists that they shall not be included in this
> world of exalted and protected womanhood.
>
> —Fannie Williams, "The Woman's Part in a Man's Business,"
>   *The Voice of the Negro*

AT THE WORLD'S CONGRESS OF REPRESENTATIVE WOMEN, HELD
from May 15 to May 22, 1893, in Chicago as part of the Columbian Exposition, Fannie Barrier Williams presented one of the
major addresses of a session titled "The Solidarity of Human Interests." That the Board of Lady Managers of the Congress presented black women as anomalies to contemporary views of blacks
is confirmed by the assertion that Williams was "selected as an
interesting representative of the colored people" (E. Davis 266).
The choice of Williams may also have been based on the persua-
siveness of her earlier arguments to the board, described by Mossell in her epideictic work on nineteenth-century black women:

> Some months ago wide publicity was given to the bril-
> liant sallies of wit and eloquence of a young Afro-Ameri-
> can woman of Chicago in appealing to the Board of Con-
> trol of the World's Columbian Exposition in behalf of the
> Negro. The grave and matter-of-fact members of the
> Commission were at first inclined to treat lightly any
> proposition to recognize the Afro-American's claim to
> representation in the World's Fair management. They
> soon found, however, that puzzling cross-questions and
> evasions awakened in this young woman such resources

of repartee, readiness of knowledge and nimbleness of logic that they were amazed into admiration and with eager unanimity embraced her arguments in a resolution of approval, and strongly recommended her appointment to some representative position. (109–110)

Whatever the motivation, Fannie Barrier Williams was there, and she delivered her address to the Congress in grand style. She was also chosen to address the World's Parliament of Religions at the exposition, delivering her speech "Religious Duty to the Negro." While she was already a prominent Chicago figure, after the delivery of these two speeches, Williams "received invitations from all parts of the country" (E. Davis 266).

Quite a bit has been recorded about Fannie Williams. She was born to a prominent Brockport, New York, family and attended the Collegiate Institute of Brockport, the New England Conservatory of Music, and the School of Fine Arts in Washington, D.C., where she taught for almost ten years. In an autobiographical essay, she describes the contrast between her early life in the North, "free, spontaneous and unhampered," and the harsh treatment she received while teaching in an ex-slave state, where for the first time she lived "life as a colored person, in all that term implies" (Williams 12–13). In 1887, she married S. Laing Williams, a Chicago attorney and protégé of Booker T. Washington. For a brief period Laing Williams shared a law office in Chicago with Ferdinand Barnett, who would later marry Ida Wells.

According to Spear, author of *Black Chicago*, Fannie Williams "soon won a reputation as an able speaker, writer, and organizer" (69). Further comments from Mossell attest to her generally well-disposed reception among black and white audiences: "Her wide and favorable acquaintance with nearly all the leading Afro-American men and women of the country, and her peculiar faculty to reach and interest influential men and women of the dominant race in presenting the peculiar needs of her people, together with her active intelligence, are destined to make Mrs. Williams a woman of conspicuous usefulness" (Mossell 112). Perhaps because of this respectability, she held a number of distinctions as the first black or the first black woman or the only woman to engage in a vari-

ety of activities. She was the first black member of the Chicago
Women's Club and the first woman to serve on the Chicago Library Board. She was also the only black woman to give remarks
at the eulogy for Susan B. Anthony at the 1907 meeting of the
National American Woman's Suffrage Association. It is within
this rhetorical context that Williams delivered her speech to the
Congress of Representative Women, "The Intellectual Progress
of the Colored Women of the United States since the Emancipation Proclamation."

Williams developed the theme of the common womanhood
shared by all women in the audience. Given the difficult circumstances under which she spoke, Williams wisely addressed simi-
larities rather than differences first, in much the same way Harper
did in her speech "We Are All Bound Up Together," delivered to
the Eleventh National Woman's Rights Convention in 1866, almost thirty years earlier. Of course, "The Solidarity of Human
Interests," the title of the session and of the first speech of the
session, established the theme of common interests. Williams,
throughout her address, argues for the common ground shared
by the women of the audience and the black women she claimed
to represent. Examining her speech reveals ways in which a rhetor
can mitigate audience hostility by emphasizing points of conver-
gence rather than divergence.

Williams opens by commending her auditors for their decision
to recognize the progress of black women: "That the discussion
of progressive womanhood in this great assemblage of the representative women of the world is considered incomplete without
some account of the colored women's status is a most noteworthy
evidence that we have not failed to impress ourselves on the higher
side of American life." Exigence is derived from the fact that little
interest has been taken in the status of black women. She dwells
at length upon what she calls a "lack of morals" among the formerly enslaved and emphasizes the need after emancipation for
learning family values and right from wrong, creating the impression that no values existed. Yet Williams's concern with moral
rectitude could well have been a reflection of the general nineteenth-century concern with morality. She proceeds to compli-

ment "those saintly women of the white race" who went South as
schoolteachers, then introduces the theme of commonality among
black and white women by pointing to the eagerness with which
black women strived "to overtake and keep pace with women
whose emancipation has been a slow and painful process for a
thousand years." Newly freed black women, she implies, are attempting to join the struggles of all women to gain their rights.
She says the character of the black women lacks "sullenness of disposition, hatefulness, and revenge against the master class," con-
cluding that these attributes "are not in the nature of our women."

In the next section she catalogs specific examples of progress
in religious diversity and in education, which serve as further evidence "that our women have the same spirit and mettle that characterize the best of American women. Everywhere they are following in the tracks of those women who are swiftest in the race
for higher knowledge." She highlights the fact that black women
are working to improve the quality of higher education for all:
"As American women generally are fighting against the nineteenth
century narrowness that still keeps women out of the higher institutions of learning, so our women are eagerly demanding the
best of education open to their race" and summarizes that they
"are ambitious to be contributors to all the great moral and intellectual forces that make for the greater weal of our common country." These women thus ask for "the same opportunity for the acquisition of all kinds of knowledge that may be accorded to other
women." Almost every paragraph, then, embodies a comparison
of some type to white women and an appeal for united action.

This call for united action in the form of participation in women's
organizations becomes most apparent in the next section, where
she places it within the context of the progress of women's groups
generally. She first asks the question, "If it be a fact that this
spirit of organization among women generally is the distinguishing mark of the nineteenth century woman, dare we ask if the
colored women of the United States have made any progress in
this respect?" She answers that black women have taken a leading
role in organizing to work "for a common destiny."

She explicitly invokes slavery as part justification for the demoralization of women. One would hope here for a denial of this received view of black women, but, as in most of her speech, her tone is not refutational. She instead emphasizes on progress and change. In this same apologetic and perhaps tongue-in-cheek manner, she states in this next paragraph, "I do not wish to disturb the serenity of this conference by suggesting why this protection [of black women] is needed and the kind of men against whom it is needed." The tone of this statement is in sharp contrast to the remarks Ida Wells made only a year earlier in her speech "Southern Horrors," where she skillfully dissects the motives behind lynching.

In the next section, Williams makes what many would characterize as a disturbing attempt to dissociate some of the Northern black women from the "non-progressive peasants" of the "'black belt' of the South." Creating a binary opposition, she claims, "It is proper to state, with as much emphasis as possible, that all questions relative to the moral progress of the colored women of America are impertinent and unjustly suggestive when they relate to the thousands of colored women in the North who were free from the vicious influences of slavery." In other words, the morality of these women, "the new generation of colored people," should not be questioned.

In the last section, she addresses the difficulty black women have had finding jobs, women with "real ability, virtue, and special talents." It is here that she provides her first and only specific example, for, as she says, "one of countless instances will show how the best as well as the meanest of American society are responsible for the special injustice to our women." In her closing paragraphs as throughout, her strongest appeal is to common interest, common needs, common consequences: "As women of a common country, with common interests, and a destiny that will certainly bring us closer to each other, we come to this altar with our contribution of hopefulness as well as with our complaints."

Closing with a final appeal for unity across race and sex, Williams relies upon one of the most effective of rhetorical strategies—establishing a strong identification with the audience. She establishes, not only through the logical appeal of her argument, but through her very presence, her powerful ethos, that surely if all women are the same, if they share a common destiny, they have a right to equal treatment.

Williams's rhetoric on behalf of black women, especially with regard to their being much maligned and having few defenders, continued well into the twentieth century.

THE INTELLECTUAL PROGRESS OF THE COLORED WOMEN OF THE UNITED STATES SINCE THE EMANCIPATION PROCLAMATION
(1893)

LESS THAN THIRTY YEARS AGO THE TERM PROGRESS AS APPLIED TO colored women of African descent in the United States would have been an anomaly. The recognition of that term to-day as appropriate is a fact full of interesting significance. That the discussion of progressive womanhood in this great assemblage of the representative women of the world is considered incomplete without some account of the colored women's status is a most noteworthy evidence that we have not failed to impress ourselves on the higher side of American life.

Less is known of our women than of any other class of Americans.

No organization of far-reaching influence for their special advancement, no conventions of women to take note of their progress, and no special literature reciting the incidents, the events, and all things interesting and instructive concerning them are to be found among the agencies directing their career. There has been no special interest in their peculiar condition as native-born American women. Their power to affect the social life of America, either for good or for ill, has excited not even a speculative interest.

Though there is much that is sorrowful, much that is wonderfully heroic, and much that is romantic in a peculiar way in their history, none of it has as yet been told as evidence of what is possible for these women. How few of the happy, prosperous, and eager living Americans can appreciate what it all means to be suddenly changed from irresponsible bondage to the responsibility of freedom and citizenship!

The distress of it all can never be told, and the pain of it all can never be felt except by the victims, and by those saintly women of the white race who for thirty years have been consecrated to the uplifting of a whole race of women from a long-enforced degradation.

The American people have always been impatient of ignorance and poverty. They believe with Emerson that "America is another word for opportunity," and for that reason success is a virtue and poverty and ignorance are inexcusable. This may account for the fact that our women have excited no general sympathy in the struggle to emancipate themselves from the demoralization of slavery. This new life of freedom, with its far-reaching responsibilities, had to be learned by these children of darkness mostly without a guide, a teacher, or a friend. In the mean vocabulary of slavery there was no definition of any of the virtues of life. The meaning of such precious terms as marriage, wife, family, and home could not be learned in a school-house. The blue-back speller, the arithmetic, and the copy-book contain no magical cures for inherited inaptitudes for the moralities. Yet it must ever be counted as one of the most wonderful things in human history how promptly and eagerly these suddenly liberated women tried to lay hold upon all that there is in human excellence. There is a touching pathos in the eagerness of these millions of new homemakers to taste the blessedness of intelligent womanhood. The path of progress in the picture is enlarged so as to bring to view these trustful and zealous students of freedom and civilization striving to overtake and keep pace with women whose emancipation has been a slow and painful process for a thousand years. The longing to be something better than they were when freedom found them has been the most notable characteristic in the development of these women. This constant striving for equality has given an upward direction to all the activities of colored women.

Freedom at once widened their vision beyond the mean cabin life of their bondage. Their native gentleness, good cheer, and hopefulness made them susceptible to those teachings that make for intelligence and righteousness. Sullenness of disposition, hatefulness, and revenge against the master class because of two centuries of ill-treatment are not in the nature of our women.

But a better view of what our women are doing and what their present status is may be had by noticing some lines of progress that are easily verifiable.

First it should be noticed that separate facts and figures relative to colored women are not easily obtainable. Among the white women of the country independence, progressive intelligence, and definite interests have done so much that nearly every fact and item illustrative of their progress and status is classified and easily accessible. Our women, on the contrary, have had no advantage of interests peculiar and distinct and separable from those of men that have yet excited public attention and kindly recognition.

In their religious life, however, our women show a progressiveness parallel in every important particular to that of white women in all Christian churches. It has always been a circumstance of the highest satisfaction to the missionary efforts of the Christian church that the colored people are so susceptible to a religion that marks the highest point of blessedness in human history.

Instead of finding witchcraft, sensual fetishes, and the coarse superstitions of savagery possessing our women, Christianity found them with hearts singularly tender, sympathetic, and fit for the reception of its doctrines. Their superstitions were not deeply ingrained, but were of the same sort and nature that characterize the devotees of the Christian faith everywhere.

While there has been but little progress toward the growing rationalism in the Christian creeds, there has been a marked advance toward a greater refinement of conception, good taste, and the proprieties. It is our young women coming out of the schools and academies that have been insisting upon a more godly and cultivated ministry. It is the young women of a new generation and new inspirations that are making tramps of the ministers who once dominated the colored church, and whose intelligence and piety were mostly in their lungs. In this new and growing religious life the colored people have laid hold of those sweeter influences of the King's Daughters, of the Christian Endeavor and Helping Hand societies, which are doing much to elevate the tone of worship and to magnify all that there is blessed in religion.

Another evidence of growing intelligence is a sense of religious discrimination among our women. Like the nineteenth century woman generally, our women find congeniality in all the creeds, from the Catholic creed to the no-creed of Emerson. There is a constant increase of this interesting variety in the religious life of our women.

Closely allied to this religious development is their progress in the work of education in schools and colleges. For thirty years education has been the magic word among the colored people of this country. That their greatest need was education in its broadest sense was understood by these people more strongly than it could be taught to them. It is the unvarying testimony of every teacher in the South that the mental development of the colored women as well as men has been little less than phenomenal. In twenty-five years, and under conditions discouraging in the extreme, thousands of our women have been educated as teachers. They have adapted themselves to the work of mentally lifting a whole race of people so eagerly and readily that they afford an apt illustration of the power of self-help. Not only have these women become good teachers in less than twenty-five years, but many of them are the prize teachers in the mixed schools of nearly every Northern city.

These women have also so fired the hearts of the race for education that colleges, normal schools, industrial schools, and universities have been reared by a generous public to meet the requirements of these eager students of intelligent citizenship. As American women generally are fighting against the nineteenth century narrowness that still keeps women out of the higher institutions of learning, so our women are eagerly demanding the best of education open to their race. They continually verify what President Rankin of Howard University recently said, "Any theory of educating the Afro-American that does not throw open the golden gates of the highest culture will fail on the ethical and spiritual side."

It is thus seen that our women have the same spirit and mettle that characterize the best of American women. Everywhere they are following in the tracks of those women who are swiftest in the race for higher knowledge.

To-day they feel strong enough to ask for but one thing, and that is the same opportunity for the acquisition of all kinds of knowledge that may be accorded to other women. This granted, in the next generation these progressive women will be found successfully occupying every field where the highest intelligence alone is admissible. In less than another generation American literature, American art, and American music will be enriched by productions having new and peculiar features of interest and excellence.

The exceptional career of our women will yet stamp itself indelibly upon the thought of this country.

American literature needs for its greater variety and its deeper soundings that which will be written into it out of the hearts of these self-emancipating women.

The great problems of social reform that are now so engaging the highest intelligence of American women will soon need for their solution the reinforcement of that new intelligence which our women are developing. In short, our women are ambitious to be contributors to all the great moral and intellectual forces that make for the greater weal of our common country.

If this hope seems too extravagant to those of you who know these women only in their humbler capacities, I would remind you that all that we hope for and will certainly achieve in authorship and practical intelligence is more than prophesied by what has already been done, and more that can be done, by hundreds of Afro-American women whose talents are now being expended in the struggle against race resistance.

The power of organized womanhood is one of the most interesting studies of modern sociology. Formerly women knew so little of each other mentally, their common interests were so sentimental and gossipy, and their knowledge of all the larger affairs of human society was so meager that organization among them, in the modern sense, was impossible. Now their liberal intelligence, their contact in all the great interests of education, and their increasing influence for good in all the great reformatory movements of the age has created in them a greater respect for each other, and furnished the elements of organization for large and splendid purposes. The highest ascendancy of woman's development has been reached when they have become mentally strong enough to find bonds of association interwoven with sympathy, loyalty, and mutual trustfulness. To-day union is the watchword of woman's onward march.

If it be a fact that this spirit of organization among women generally is the distinguishing mark of the nineteenth century woman, dare we ask if the colored women of the United States have made any progress in this respect?

For peculiar and painful reasons the great lessons of fraternity and altruism are hard for the colored women to learn. Emancipation found the colored Americans of the South with no sentiments of association. It will be admitted that race misfortune could scarcely go further when the terms fraternity, friendship, and unity had no meaning for its men and women.

If within thirty years they have begun to recognize the blessed significance of these vital terms of human society, confidence in their social development should be strengthened. In this important work of bringing the race together to know itself and to unite in work for a common destiny, the women have taken a leading part.

Benevolence is the essence of most of the colored women's organizations. The humane side of their natures has been cultivated to recognize the duties they owe to the sick, the indigent and ill-fortuned. No church, school, or charitable institution for the special use of colored people has been allowed to languish or fail when the associated efforts of the women could save it.

It is highly significant and interesting to note that these women, whose hearts have been wrung by all kinds of sorrows, are abundantly manifesting those gracious qualities of heart that characterize women of the best type. These kinder sentiments arising from mutual interests that are lifting our women into purer and tenderer relationship to each other, and are making the meager joys and larger griefs of our conditions known to each other, have been a large part of their education.

The hearts of Afro-American women are too warm and too large for race hatred. Long suffering has so chastened them that they are developing a special sense of sympathy for all who suffer and fail of justice. All the associated interests of church, temperance, and social reform in which American women are winning distinction can be wonderfully advanced when our women shall be welcomed *as co-workers*, and estimated solely by what they are worth to the moral elevation of all the people.

I regret the necessity of speaking to the question of the moral progress of our women, because the morality of our home life has been commented upon so disparagingly and meanly that we are placed in the unfortunate position of being defenders of our name.

It is proper to state, with as much emphasis as possible, that all questions relative to the moral progress of the colored women of America are impertinent and unjustly suggestive when they relate to the thousands of colored women in the North who were free from the vicious influences of slavery. They are also meanly suggestive as regards thousands of our women in the South whose force of character enabled them to escape the slavery taints of immorality. The question of the moral progress of colored women in the United States has force and meaning in this discussion only so far as it tells the story of how the once-enslaved women have been struggling for twenty-five years to emancipate themselves from the demoralization of their enslavement.

While I duly appreciate the offensiveness of all references to American slavery, it is unavoidable to charge to that system every moral imperfection that mars the character of the colored American. The whole life and power of slavery depended upon an enforced degradation of everything human in the slaves. The slave code recognized only animal distinctions between the sexes, and ruthlessly ignored those ordinary separations that belong to the social state.

It is a great wonder that two centuries of such demoralization did not work a complete extinction of all the moral instincts. But the recuperative power of these women to regain their moral instincts and to establish a respectable relationship to American womanhood is among the earlier evidences of their moral ability to rise above their conditions. In spite of a cursed heredity that bound them to the lowest social level, in spite of everything that is unfortunate and unfavorable, these women have continually shown an increasing degree of teachableness as to the meaning of woman's relationship to man.

Out of this social purification and moral uplift have come a chivalric sentiment and regard from the young men of the race that give to the young women a new sense of protection. I do not wish to disturb the serenity of this conference by suggesting why this protection is needed and the kind of men against whom it is needed.

It is sufficient for us to know that the daughters of women who thirty years ago were not allowed to be modest, not allowed to follow the instincts of moral rectitude, who could cry for protection to no living man, have so elevated the moral tone of their social life that new and purer standards of personal worth have been created, and new ideals of womanhood, instinct with grace and delicacy, are everywhere recognized and emulated.

This moral regeneration of a whole race of women is no idle sentiment—it is a serious business; and everywhere there is witnessed a feverish anxiety to be free from the mean suspicions that have so long underestimated the character strength of our women.

These women are not satisfied with the unmistakable fact that moral progress has been made, but they are fervently impatient and stirred by a sense of outrage under the vile imputations of a diseased public opinion.

Loves that are free from the dross of coarseness, affections that are unsullied, and a proper sense of all the sanctities of human intercourse felt by thousands of these women all over the land plead for the recognition of their fitness to be judged, not by the standards of slavery, but by the higher standards of freedom and of twenty-five years of education, culture, and moral contact.

The moral aptitudes of our women are just as strong and just as weak as those of any other American women with like advantages of intelligence and environment.

It may now perhaps be fittingly asked, What mean all these evidences of mental, social, and moral progress of a class of American women of whom you know so little? Certainly you can not be indifferent to the growing needs and importance of women who are demonstrating their intelligence and capacity for the highest privileges of freedom.

The most important thing to be noted is the fact that the colored people of America have reached a distinctly new era in their career so quickly that the American mind has scarcely had time to recognize the fact, and adjust itself to the new requirements of the people in all things that pertain to citizenship.

Thirty years ago public opinion recognized no differences in the colored race. To our great misfortune public opinion has changed but slightly. History is full of examples of the great injustice resulting from the perversity of public opinion, and its tardiness in recognizing new conditions.

It seems to daze the understanding of the ordinary citizen that there are thousands of men and women everywhere among us who in twenty-five years have progressed as far away from the non-progressive peasants of the "black belt" of the South as the highest social life in New England is above the lowest levels of American civilization.

This general failure of the American people to know the new generation of colored people, and to recognize this important change in them, is the cause of more injustice to our women than can well be estimated. Further progress is everywhere seriously hindered by this ignoring of their improvement.

Our exclusion from the benefits of the fair play sentiment of the country is little less than a crime against the ambitions and aspirations of a whole race of women. The American people are but repeating the common folly of history in thus attempting to repress the yearnings of progressive humanity.

In the item of employment colored women bear a distressing burden of mean and unreasonable discrimination. A Southern teacher of thirty years' experience in the South writes that "one million possibilities of good through black womanhood all depend upon an opportunity to make a living."

It is almost literally true that, except teaching in colored schools and menial work, colored women can find no employment in this free America. They are the only women in the country for whom real ability, virtue, and special talents count for nothing when they become applicants for respectable employment. Taught everywhere in ethics and social economy that merit always wins, colored women carefully prepare themselves for all kinds of occupation only to meet with stern refusal, rebuff, and disappointment. One of countless instances will show how the best as well as the meanest of American society are responsible for the special injustice to our women.

Not long ago I presented the case of a bright young woman to a well-known bank president of Chicago, who was in need of a thoroughly competent stenographer and typewriter. The president was fully satisfied with the young woman as exceptionally qualified for the position, and manifested much pleasure in commending her to the directors for appointment, and at the same time disclaimed that there could be any opposition on account of the slight tinge of African blood that identified her as a colored woman. Yet, when the matter was brought before the directors for action, these mighty men of money and business, these men whose prominence in all the great interests of the city would seem to lift them above all narrowness and foolishness, scented the African taint, and at once bravely came to the rescue of the bank and of society by dashing the hopes of this capable yet helpless young woman. No other question but that of color determined the action of these men, many of whom are probably foremost members of the humane society and heavy contributors to foreign missions and church extension work.

This question of employment for the trained talents of our women is a most serious one. Refusal of such employment because of color belies every maxim of justice and fair play. Such refusal takes the blessed meaning out of all the teachings of our civilization, and sadly confuses our conceptions of what is just, humane, and moral.

Can the people of this country afford to single out the women of a whole race of people as objects of their special contempt? Do these women not belong to a race that has never faltered in its support of the country's flag in every war since Attucks fell in Boston's streets?

Are they not the daughters of men who have always been true as steel against treason to everything fundamental and splendid in the republic? In short, are these women not as thoroughly American in all the circumstances of citizenship as the best citizens of our country?

If it be so, are we not justified in a feeling of desperation against that peculiar form of Americanism that shows respect for our women as servants and contempt for them when they become women of culture? We have never been taught to understand why the unwritten law of chivalry, protection, and fair play that are everywhere the conservators of women's welfare must exclude every woman of a dark complexion.

We believe that the world always needs the influence of every good and capable woman, and this rule recognizes no exceptions based on complexion. In their complaint against hindrances to their employment colored women ask for no special favors.

They are even willing to bring to every position fifty per cent more of ability than is required of any other class of women. They plead for opportunities untrammeled by prejudice. They plead for the right of the individual to be judged, not by tradition and race estimate, but by the present evidences of individual worth. We believe this country is large enough and the opportunities for all kinds of success are great enough to afford our women a fair chance to earn a respectable living, and to win every prize within the reach of their capabilities.

Another, and perhaps more serious, hindrance to our women is that nightmare known as "social equality." The term equality is the most inspiring word in the vocabulary of citizenship. It expresses the leveling quality in all the splendid possibilities of American life. It is this idea of equality that has made room in this country for all kinds and conditions of men, and made personal merit the supreme requisite for all kinds of achievement.

When the colored people became citizens, and found it written deep in the organic law of the land that they too had the right to life, liberty, and the pursuit of happiness, they were at once suspected of wishing to interpret this maxim of equality as meaning social equality.

Everywhere the public mind has been filled with constant alarm lest in some way our women shall approach the social sphere of the dominant race in this country. Men and women, wise and perfectly sane in all things else, become instantly unwise and foolish at the remotest suggestion of social contact with colored men and women. At every turn in our lives we meet this fear, and are humiliated by its aggressiveness and meanness. If we seek the sanctities of religion, the enlightenment of the university, the honors of politics, and the natural recreations of our common country, the social equality alarm is instantly given, and our aspirations are insulted. "Beware of social equality with the colored American" is thus written on all places, sacred or profane, in this blessed land of liberty. The most discouraging and demoralizing effect of this false sentiment concerning us is that it utterly ignores individual merit and discredits the sensibilities of intelligent womanhood. The sorrows and heartaches of a whole race of women seem to be matters of no concern to the people who so dread the social possibilities of these colored women.

On the other hand, our women have been wonderfully indifferent and unconcerned about the matter. The dread inspired by the growing intelligence of colored women has interested us almost to the point of amusement. It has given to colored women a new sense of importance to witness how easily their emancipation and steady advancement is disturbing all classes of American people. It may not be a discouraging circumstance that colored women can command some sort of attention, even though they be misunderstood. We believe in the law of reaction, and it is reasonably certain that the forces of intelligence and character being developed in our women will yet change mistrustfulness into confidence and contempt into sympathy and respect. It will soon appear to those who are not hopelessly monomaniacs on the subject that the colored people are in no way responsible for the social equality nonsense. We shall yet be credited with knowing better than our enemies that social equality can neither be enforced by law nor prevented by oppression. Though not philosophers, we long since learned that equality before the law, equality in the best sense of that term under our institutions, is totally different from social equality.

We know, without being exceptional students of history, that the social relationship of the two races will be adjusted equitably in spite of all fear and injustice, and that there is a social gravitation in human affairs that eventually overwhelms and crushes into nothingness all resistance based on prejudice and selfishness.

Our chief concern in this false social sentiment is that it attempts to hinder our further progress toward the higher spheres of womanhood. On account of it, young colored women of ambition and means are compelled in many instances to leave the country for training and education in the salons and studios of Eu-

rope. On many of the railroads of this country women of refinement and culture are driven like cattle into human cattle-cars lest
the occupying of an individual seat paid for in a first-class car may
result in social equality. This social quarantine on all means of
travel in certain parts of the country is guarded and enforced more
rigidly against us than the quarantine regulations against cholera.

Without further particularizing as to how this social question
opposes our advancement, it may be stated that the contentions of
colored women are in kind like those of other American women
for greater freedom of development. Liberty to be all that we can
be, without artificial hindrances, is a thing no less precious to us
than to women generally.

We come before this assemblage of women feeling confident
that our progress has been along high levels and rooted deeply in
the essentials of intelligent humanity. We are so essentially American in speech, in instincts, in sentiments and destiny that the things
that interest you equally interest us.

We believe that social evils are dangerously contagious. The
fixed policy of persecution and injustice against a class of women
who are weak and defenseless will be necessarily hurtful to the
cause of all women. Colored women are becoming more and
more a part of the social forces that must help to determine the
questions that so concern women generally. In this Congress we
ask to be known and recognized for what we are worth. If it be
the high purpose of these deliberations to lessen the resistance to
woman's progress, you can not fail to be interested in our struggles against the many oppositions that harass us.

Women who are tender enough in heart to be active in humane
societies, to be foremost in all charitable activities, who are loving
enough to unite Christian womanhood everywhere against the
sin of intemperance, ought to be instantly concerned in the plea
of colored women for justice and humane treatment. Women of
the dominant race can not afford to be responsible for the wrongs
we suffer, since those who do injustice can not escape a certain
penalty.

But there is no wish to overstate the obstacles to colored women
or to picture their status as hopeless. There is no disposition to
take our place in this Congress as faultfinders or suppliants for

mercy. As women of a common country, with common interests, and a destiny that will certainly bring us closer to each other, we come to this altar with our contribution of hopefulness as well as with our complaints.

When you learn that womanhood everywhere among us is blossoming out into greater fullness of everything that is sweet, beautiful, and good in women; when you learn that the bitterness of our experience as citizen-women has not hardened our finer feelings of love and pity for our enemies; when you learn that fierce opposition to the widening spheres of our employment has not abated the aspirations of our women to enter successfully into all the professions and arts open only to intelligence, and that everywhere in the wake of enlightened womanhood our women are seen and felt for the good they diffuse, this Congress will at once see the fullness of our fellowship, and help us to avert the arrows of prejudice that pierce the soul because of the color of our bodies.

If the love of humanity more than the love of races and sex shall pulsate throughout all the grand results that shall issue to the world from this parliament of women, women of African descent in the United States will for the first time begin to feel the sweet release from the blighting thrall of prejudice.

The colored women, as well as all women, will realize that the inalienable right to life, liberty, and the pursuit of happiness is a maxim that will become more blessed in its significance when the hand of woman shall take it from its sepulture in books and make it the gospel of every-day life and the unerring guide in the relations of all men, women, and children.

7 VICTORIA EARLE MATTHEWS (1861–1907)

> If there had been no other awakening than this, if this
> woman who had stood upon the auction block possessed
> of no rights that a white man was bound to respect, and
> none which he did respect, if there had been no other
> awakening of the Afro-American woman than this, that
> she made a home for her race, an abiding place for hus-
> band, and son, and daughter, it would be glory enough to
> embalm her memory in song and story.
>
> —Victoria Earle Matthews, "The Awakening of the Afro-
>   American Woman"

ON JUNE 1, 1895, JOSEPHINE ST. PIERRE RUFFIN, A BOSTON
activist in the women's movement and one of the organizers of
the 1892 testimonial for Ida B. Wells, issued a call for black women
to gather in defense of themselves. This call was in response to
an open letter from the president of the Missouri Press Association, John W. Jacks, denigrating black women, claiming that
they were "wholly devoid of morality and that they were prosti-
tutes, thieves and liars" (Wesley 28). The letter had been sent to
Florence Balgarnie of the British Anti-Lynching Committee in
rebuttal to Ida Wells's accounts of lynching in the South. In her
call Ruffin admonishes: "Read this document [a copy of Jacks's
letter] carefully and use it discriminately and decide if it be not
time for us to stand before the world and declare ourselves and
our principles. The time is short but everything is ripe and remember, earnest women can do anything" (Wesley 29). As a result
of Ruffin's call, the First Congress of Colored Women convened
July 29, 1895, in Boston.[1] Victoria Earle Matthews's speech "The
Value of Race Literature" was delivered at this conference. Matthews's own life story reflected the challenge Ruffin placed before
these women.

Victoria Earle was born in Fort Valley, Georgia, May 27, 1861,
to William and Caroline Smith, both slaves. About 1873, her mother

took Victoria and three siblings to live with her in New York. Like Frances Harper, Earle took advantage of her first city job in a home with a library to read as much as she could. According to one biographer, "by means of lectures, special studies, constant contact with trained persons, she gratified to some extent her thirst for knowledge and became in spite of untoward circumstances an educated, cultured woman" (Brown 209–210). At eighteen, Earle married William Matthews; they had one son who died at sixteen.

Matthews was active as a journalist, writing for such publications as the *Sunday Mercury*, *Phonographic World*, the *Detroit Plaindealer*, the *New York Age*, and the *A.M.E. Church Review*. Her published works include *Black Belt Diamonds* (1898), a small collection of Booker T. Washington's speeches, and a short story, "Aunt Lindy: A Story Founded on Real Life" (1893). She was also a pioneer in the black women's club movement. In 1892, Matthews spearheaded the formation of the Women's Loyal Union of New York and Brooklyn, one of the first black women's organizations in the country, and became its first president. Like Ruffin, she was also a leading organizer of the testimonial to honor Ida Wells.

During her travels South, Matthews used her Caucasian features to enter segregated establishments where she uncovered methods by which Southern black women became victims of unethical employment practices. Her interest in the plight of young black women migrating to the North led to the founding of the White Rose Mission Industrial Association to provide them with training and care. This mission eventually became part of the National Urban League. Speaking on the second day of the Boston conference, held in Berekely Hall, Matthews shared the podium with Mrs. Booker T. Washington, abolitionist William Lloyd Garrison, and T. Thomas Fortune, newspaper publisher, along with other prominent leaders. Additional topics addressed on that second day included "A Plea for Justice," "Industrial Training," "Individual Work for Mental Elevation," and "Political Equity."

Given this context and occasion, Matthews's speech "Value of Race Literature" was, in many respects, a curious response. The opening day's speeches, including Ruffin's "Address of the President" and Anna Cooper's "Need of Organization," called on the women to organize to fight against the maligning of black women. Ruffin's speech set the tone by admonishing, "This conference will not be what I expect if it does not show the wisdom, indeed the absolute necessity of a national organization of our women" (E. Davis 19). Ruffin's other concern was that black women's reputations be restored: "It is 'meet, right, and our bounden duty' to stand forth and declare ourselves and principles, to teach an ignorant and suspicious world that our aims and interests are identical with those of all good aspiring women" (E. Davis 18).

With these two declared goals for the conference resounding in the ears of the participants, Matthews delivered an epideictic oration, as its title signifies. Aristotle divided the kinds of oratory according to purpose into forensic, concentrating on past events to make judicial decisions, deliberative, concerned with the best possible course of future action, and epideictic, with its focus on the positive or negative features of current conditions (*Rhetoric* 1.3). To some extent all of the speeches included in this anthology contain a section in which the accomplishments of the race are applauded. But in Matthews's speech, the primary purpose is epideictic. The first portion condemns the negative portrayals of African-Americans in writing by white authors. The second part praises the writings of blacks who have pushed against these negative stereotypes. As such, Matthews's speech could seem to be somewhat removed from the urgency of the occasion; yet it was, in a way, quite appropriate. It exhorted the women to write their own stories and to project their own positive images, since clearly no one else would do it for them. By praising the past and current literary accomplishments of African-Americans, Matthews's speech also served a deliberative purpose. In effect, she was saying to her auditors, look at what we are capable of producing; we can do more.

Further, it was natural for her to speak on a subject that had always sparked her intellect. As one biographer points out:

Long before the interest in Race Literature became general, she was an enthusiast on the subject and placed in

the White Rose Home a choice collection of books written by and about the Negro in America. . . . The books in
this library were used by Mrs. Matthews as a basis for her
class in Race History. . . . She sought eagerly, almost im-
petuously, to impart to a group of intelligent young men
and women the knowledge of the work and worth of the
men and women of their race—a knowledge with which
she was completely saturated. (Brown 215–216)

Because the speech is filled with references to nineteenth-century authors and works that may no longer be familiar to late-
twentieth-century readers, some have here been briefly identified
in notes. Yet, Matthews's ultimate goal was probably to impress
her audience with the volume and range of material rather than to
highlight specific authors or works. She wanted to make the point
that examples of damaging, race-biased literature and positive race
representations both were numerous. This point is no doubt made
without the identifying notes; they are included mainly for the
curious.

The second speech included here, "The Awakening of the Afro-
American Woman," was delivered two years later, in 1897, at
the Annual Convention of the Society of Christian Endeavor in
San Francisco. The society was a Protestant, interdenominational
young people's movement established in 1881 by Francis E. Clark
of Portland, Maine (Malloch 90). When Matthews addressed the
convention, the society, representing the beginning of youth ac-
tivism in the Protestant and Anglican churches, included a membership of over a million and a half (Chalmers 45). Matthews,
at the time thirty-six years old, may have been invited to speak
because of her prominence in black women's organizations and
her charitable work on behalf of the young men and women associated with the White Rose Mission.

Matthews's appeal in "The Awakening" is to the common Christianity shared by the members of her audience and the members
of the black community. The adjective "Christian" is applied to
various concepts—including nation, womanhood, homes, work,
virtues, law, opinion, and government—over twenty times in

what was probably a twenty-minute speech. This is in marked contrast to "The Value of Race Literature," a much longer speech, which gives only five references to Christianity. Clearly, Matthews was aware of the differing appeals needed to reach an audience of prominent black women assembled in response to continued disparagement, on the one hand, and a group of young white Christian men and women, far removed from such a crisis, on the other.

Also striking is her development of the metaphor of growth. She compares the progress of the black woman after emancipation to the budding of a flower. This is the same metaphor Anna Cooper invokes in her speech "Womanhood a Vital Element in the Regeneration and Progress of a Race" (see chapter 4). Cooper, also extolling the black woman, describes her as a "delicate plantlet," declaring that there must be "life in the plant germ" if the race is to thrive. Matthews's plant imagery also evokes the structure of Chalmers's 1893 book *The Juvenile Revival; or The Philosophy of the Christian Endeavor Movement*, which develops around this growth metaphor with chapters titled "The Soil," "The Season," "The Seed," "The Blade," "The Ear," and "The Full Corn"; Matthews may have been familiar with the work. Also building upon this metaphor, Matthews retraces the accomplishments of women whose roots stem from the soil of slavery and who, in spite of these degrading beginnings, can be credited with establishing Christian homes, contributing to economic stability and educational advancement, supporting black church memberships, and motivating a new generation of educated black women to organize.

She makes a direct appeal to the "Christian womanhood" in her audience to push for the repeal of the laws in some states against marriage between persons of different races, claiming that such laws are "the greatest demoralizing forces with which our womanhood has to contend." Matthews ends with a cataloging of needs—removal of separate train car regulations, reformation of the penal system, care for infants, the sick and the elderly. She identifies these as issues that should be of common concern to "Christian men and women everywhere."

NOTE

1. The women used this exigence to organize the National Federation of Afro-American Women, uniting thirty-six clubs in twelve states. This organization merged in 1896 with the League of Colored Women into the National Association of Colored Women (NACW) with Mary Church Terrell as its first president.

THE VALUE OF RACE LITERATURE: AN ADDRESS DELIVERED AT THE FIRST CONGRESS OF COLORED WOMEN OF THE UNITED STATES (1895)

BY RACE LITERATURE, WE MEAN ORDINARILY ALL THE WRITINGS emanating from a distinct class—not necessarily race matter; but a general collection of what has been written by the men and women of that Race: History, Biographies, Scientific Treatises, Sermons, Addresses, Novels, Poems, Books of Travel, miscellaneous essays and the contributions to magazines and newspapers.

Literature, according to Webster, is learning; acquaintance with books or letters: the collective body of literary productions, embracing the entire results of knowledge and fancy, preserved in writing, *also the whole body of literature,* productions or writings upon any given subject, or in reference to a particular science, a branch of knowledge, as the Literature of Biblical Customs, the Literature of Chemistry, Etc.

In the light of this definition, many persons may object to the term, Race Literature, questioning seriously the need, doubting if there be any, or indeed whether there can be a Race Literature in a country like ours apart from the general American Literature. Others may question the correctness of the term American Literature, since our civilization in its essential features is a reproduction of all that is most desirable in the civilizations of the Old World. English being the language of America, they argue in favor of the general term, English Literature.

While I have great respect for the projectors of this theory, yet it is a limited definition; it does not express the idea in terms sufficiently clear.

The conditions which govern the people of African descent in the United States have been and still are, such as create a very

Published with permission of the Moorland-Spingarn Research Center, Howard University.

marked difference in the limitations, characteristics, aspirations and ambitions of this class of people, in decidedly strong contrast with the more or less powerful races which dominate it.

Laws were enacted denying and restricting their mental development in such pursuits, which engendered servility and begot ox-like endurance; and though statutes were carefully, painstakingly prepared by the most advanced and learned American jurists to perpetuate ignorance, yet they were powerless to keep all the race out from the Temple of Learning. Many though in chains mastered the common rudiments and others possessing talent of higher order—like the gifted Phyllis Wheatley, who dared to express her meditations in poetic elegance which won recognition in England and America, from persons distinguished in letters and statesmanship—dared to seek the sources of knowledge and wield a pen.

While oppressive legislation, aided by grossly inhuman customs, successfully retarded all general efforts toward improvement, the race suffered physically and mentally under a great wrong, an appalling evil, in contrast with which the religious caste prejudice of India appears as a glimmering torch to a vast consuming flame.

The prejudice of color! Not condition, not character, not capacity for artistic development, not the possibility of emerging from savagery into Christianity, not these, but the "Prejudice of Color." Washington Irving's *Life of Columbus* contains a translation from the contemporaries of Las Casas, in which this prejudice is plainly evident.[1] Since our reception on this continent, men have cried out against this inhuman prejudice; granting that, a man may improve his condition, accumulate wealth, become wise

1. Washington Irving (1783–1859) was the author of *History of the Life and Voyages of Christopher Columbus* (1828), a detailed account of Spanish life and history, which was said to be naively interpreted. Bartolomé de Las Casas (1474–1566) was a Spanish missionary and historian who worked to improve the maltreatment of South American Indians by proposing that Africans be enslaved instead. (See John Hope Franklin, *From Slavery to Freedom*, 3rd ed., for a discussion of Las Casas's role in the perpetuation of slavery.)

and upright, merciful and just as an infidel or Christian, but they despair because he can not change his color, as if it were possible for the victim to change his organic structure, and impossible for the oppressor to change his wicked heart.

But all this impious wrong has made a Race Literature a possibility, even a necessity to dissipate the odium conjured up by the term "colored" persons, not originally perhaps designed to humiliate, but unfortunately still used to express not only an inferior order, but to accentuate and call unfavorable attention to the most ineradicable difference between the races.

So well was this understood and deplored by liberal minded men, regardless of affiliation, that the editor of "Freedom's Journal," published in New York City in 1827, the first paper published in this country by Americans of African descent, calls special attention to this prejudice by quoting from the great Clarkson, where he speaks of a master not only looking with disdain upon a slave's features, but hating his very color.[2]

The effect of this unchristian disposition was like the merciless scalpel about the very heart of the people, a sword of Damocles, at all times hanging above and threatening all that makes life worth living. Why they should not develop and transmit stealthy, vicious and barbaric natures under such conditions, is a question that able metaphysicians, ethnologists and scientists will, most probably in the future, investigate with a view of solving what to-day is considered in all quarters a profound mystery, the Negro's many-sided, happy, hopeful, enduring character.

Future investigations may lead to the discovery of what to-day seems lacking, what has deformed the manhood and womanhood in the Negro. What is bright, hopeful and encouraging is in reality the source of an original school of race literature, of racial psychology, of potent possibilities, an amalgam needed for this great American race of the future.

Dr. Dvorak claims this for the original Negro melodies of the

---

2. *Freedom's Journal* was owned and edited by John Russwurm and Samuel E. Cornish. Thomas Clarkson (1760–1846) was an English abolitionist associated with Wilberforce University. He wrote articles criticizing the British colonies' involvement in the slave trade.

South, as every student of music is well aware.[3] On this subject
he says,

> I am now satisfied that the future music of this conti-
> nent must be founded upon what are called the Negro
> melodies. This can be the foundation of a serious and
> original school of composition to be developed in the
> United States.
>
> When I first came here, I was impressed with this idea,
> and it has developed into a settled conviction. The beauti-
> ful and varied themes are the product of the soil. *They are
> American, they are the folk songs of America, and our com-
> posers must turn to them.* All of the great musicians have
> borrowed from the songs of the common people.
>
> Beethoven's most charming *scherzo* is based upon what
> might now be considered a skilfully handled Negro
> melody. I have myself gone to the simple half-forgotten
> tunes of the Bohemian peasants for hints in my most seri-
> ous work. Only in this way can a musician express the
> true sentiment of a people. He gets into touch with com-
> mon humanity of the country.
>
> *In the Negro melodies of America I discover all that is
> needed for a great and noble school of music. They are pa-
> thetic, tender, passionate and melancholy, solemn, religious,
> bold, merry, gay, gracious, or what you will. It is music that
> suits itself to any work or any purpose. There is nothing in
> the whole range of composition that cannot find a thematic
> source here.*

When the literature of our race is developed, it will of necessity be different in all essential points of greatness, true heroism
and real Christianity from what we may at the present time, for
convenience, call American Literature. When some master hand

---

3. Anton Dvorak (1841–1904) was a Czech composer noted for his
use of Slavic folk material in his compositions. He is know best for his
symphony *From the New World*, which incorporated many of the melodies of Negro spirituals.

writes the stories as Dr. Dvorak has caught the melodies, when, amid the hearts of the people, there shall live a George Eliott [sic], moving this human world by the simple portrayal of the scenes of our ordinary existence; or when the pure, ennobling touch of a black Hannah More shall rightly interpret our unappreciated contribution to Christianity and make it into universal literature, such writers will attain and hold imperishable fame.[4]

The novelists most read at the present time in this country find a remunerative source for their doubtful literary productions based upon the wrongly interpreted and too often grossly exaggerated frailties. This is patent to all intelligent people. The Negro need not envy such reputation, nor feel lost at not revelling in its ill-gotten wealth or repute. We are the only people most distinctive from those who have civilized and governed this country, who have become typical Americans, and we rank next to the Indians in originality of soil, and yet remain a distinct people.

In this connection, Joseph Wilson, in the "Black Phalanx," says: "The Negro race is the only race that has ever come in contact with the European race that has proved itself able to withstand its atrocities and oppression. All others like the Indians whom they could not make subservient to their use they have destroyed."[5]

Prof. Sampson in his "Mixed Races" says, "The American Negro is a new race, and is not the direct descent of any people that has ever flourished."

On this supposition, and relying upon finely developed, native imaginative powers, and humane tendencies, I base my expectation that our Race Literature when developed will not only compare favorably with many, but will stand out preeminent, not only in the limited history of colored people, but in the broader field of universal literature.

Though Race Literature be founded upon the traditionary history of a people, yet its fullest and largest development ought not to be circumscribed by the narrow limits of race or creed, for the simple reason that literature in its loftiest development reaches

4. George Eliot (Mary Ann Evans) (1819–1880) and Hannah More (1745–1835) were English philanthropists and novelists who wrote on moral and religious subjects.

5. Joseph T. Wilson (1836–1891) wrote *The Black Phalanx*, a history of the negro in the Civil War, in 1888.

out to the utmost limits of soul enlargement and outstrips all earthly limitations. Our history and individuality as a people, not only provides material for masterly treatment; but would seem to make a Race Literature a necessity as an outlet for the unnaturally suppressed inner lives which our people have been compelled to lead.

The literature of any people of varied nationality who have won a place in the literature of the world, presents certain cardinal points. French literature for instance, is said to be "not the wisest, not the weightiest, not certainly the purest and loftiest, but by odds the most brilliant and the most interesting literature in the world."

Ours, when brought out, and we must admit in reverence to truth that, as yet, we have done nothing distinctive, but may when we have built upon our own individuality, win a place by the simplicity of the story, thrown into strong relief by the multiplicity of its dramatic situations; the spirit of romance, and even tragedy, shadowy and as yet ill-defined, but from which our race on this continent can never be disassociated.

When the foundations of such a literature shall have been properly laid, the benefit to be derived will be at once apparent. There will be a revelation to our people, and it will enlarge our scope, make us better known wherever real lasting culture exists, will undermine and utterly drive out the traditional Negro in dialect,—the subordinate, the servant as the type representing a race whose numbers are now far into the millions. It would suggest to the world the wrong and contempt with which the lion viewed the picture that the hunter and a famous painter besides, had drawn of the King of the Forest.

As a matter of history, the only high-type Negro that has been put before the American people by a famous writer, is the character Dred founded upon the deeds of Nat Turner, in Mrs. Stowe's novel. [6]

Except the characters sketched by the writers of folk-lore, I

6. Harriet Beecher Stowe's novel *Dred: A Tale of the Great Dismal Swamp* (1856) was probably based on the insurrections of Denmark Vesey and Nat Turner. *Dred* is about a biblical prophet of wrath and judgment who leads a group of fugitive slaves into a swamp to prepare to strike out in vengeance upon a sign from God.

know of none more representative of the spirit of the writers of
to-day, wherein is infiltrated in the public mind that false sense
of the Negro's meaning of inalienable rights, so far as actual practice is concerned, than is found in a story in "Harper's Magazine"
some years ago. Here a pathetic picture is drawn of a character
generally known as the typical "Darkey."

The man, old and decrepit, had labored through long years to
pay for an humble cabin and garden patch; in fact, he had paid
double and treble the original price, but dashing "Marse Wilyum"
quieted his own conscience by believing, so the writer claimed,
that the old Darkey should be left free to pay him all he felt the
cabin was worth to him. The old man looked up to him, trusted
him implicitly, and when he found at last he had been deceived,
the moment he acknowledged to himself that "Marse Wilyum"
had cheated him, a dejected listlessness settled upon him, an expression weak and vacant came in his dull eyes and hung around his
capacious but characterless mouth, an exasperatingly meek smile
trembled upon his features, and casting a helpless look around
the cabin that he thought his own, nay, knew it was, with drag-
ging steps he left the place! "Why did you not stand out for your
rights?" a sympathizing friend questioned some years afterwards.
To this the writer makes the old man say:

"Wid white folks dat's de way, but wid niggers it's dif'unt."

Here the reader is left to infer whatever his or her predilection
will incline to accept, as to the meaning of the old man's words.
The most general view is that the old man had no manhood, not
the sense, nothing to even suggest to his inner conscience aught
that could awaken a comprehension of the word man, much less its
rightful price; no moral responsibility, no spirit or, as the Negro-
hating Mark Twain would say, no capacity of kicking at real or
imaginary wrongs, which in his estimation makes the superior
clan. In a word, there was nothing within the old man's range of
understanding to make him feel his inalienable rights.

We know the true analysis of the old man's words was that
faith, once destroyed, can never be regained, and the blow to his
faith in the individual and the wound to his honest esteem so overwhelming, rendered it out of the question to engage further with
a fallen idol.

With one sweep of mind he had seen the utter futility of even hoping for justice from a people who would take advantage of an aged honest man. That is the point, and this reveals a neglected subject for analytical writers to dissect in the interest of truth the real meaning of the so-called cowardice, self-negation and lack of responsibility so freely referred to by those in positions calculated to make lasting impressions on the public, that by custom scoffs at the meaning introduced in Mrs. Stowe's burning words, when she repeated a question before answering;—"What can any individual do?" "There is one thing every individual can do. They can see to it that they feel right—an atmosphere of sympathetic influence encircles every human being; and the man or woman who feels strongly, healthily and justly on the great interests of humanity, is a constant benefactor to the human race."

Think of the moral status of the Negro, that Mr. Ridpath in his history degrades before the world. Consider the political outline of the Negro, sketched with extreme care in "Bryce's Commonwealth," and the diatribes of Mr. Froude. From these, turn to the play, where impressions are made upon a heterogeneous assemblage—Mark Twain's "Pudd'n Head Wilson," which Beaumount Fletcher claims as "among the very best of those productions which gives us hope for a distinctive American drama."[7]

In this story we have education and fair environment attended by the most deplorable results, an educated octoroon is made out to be a most despicable, cowardly villain. "The one compensation for all this," my friend, Professor Greener wittily remarks, "is that the 'white nigger' in the story though actually a pure white man, is indescribably worse in all his characteristics than the 'real

7. John Clarke Ridpath (1840–1900) was an educator and historian of racial history. Matthews is probably referring to his historical account of man in *Great Races of Mankind*. James Bryce (1838–1922) was an English historian and diplomat. He wrote *The American Commonwealth* (1888), a political and social survey of American society. James Anthony Froude (1818–1894) was an English historian heavily involved in religious order. He was considered careless in his use of facts and transcripts relating to people's lives. Mark Twain (Samuel Langhorne Clemens) (1835–1910) was the author of *The Tragedy of Pudd'nhead Wilson* (1894), a novel centered on miscegenation and the influence of heredity and environment on one's development.

nigger,' using the vernacular of the play, was ever known to be, and just here Mark Twain unconsciously avenges the Negro while trying his best to disparage him."[8]

In "Imperative Duty," Mr. Howells laboriously establishes for certain minds, the belief that the Negro possesses an Othello like charm in his ignorance which education and refinement destroys, or at best makes repulsive.[9]

In explaining why Dr. Olney loves Rhoda, whose training was imparted by good taste, refined by wealth, and polished by foreign travel, he says:

> It was the elder world, the beauty of antiquity which appealed to him in the luster and sparkle of this girl, and the *remote taint* of her servile and savage origin, *gave her a fascination* which refuses to let itself be put in words, it was the grace of a limp, the occult, indefinable, lovableness of deformity, but transcending these by its allurements, in indefinite degree, and going for the reason of its effect deep into the mysterious places of being, where the spirit and animal meet and part in us.
>
> The mood was of his emotional nature alone, it sought and could have won no justification from the moral sense which indeed it simply submerged, and blotted out for all time.

All this tergiversation and labored explanation of how a white man came to love a girl with a remote tinge of Negro blood! But he must have recourse to this tortuous jugglery of words, because one of his characters in the story had taken pains to assert, "That so far as society in the society sense is concerned we have frankly simplified the matter, and no more consort with the Negroes than we do with lower animals, so that one would be quite as likely to meet a cow or a horse in an American drawing-room, as a person

8. Richard Theodore Greener (1844–1922) was an educator and lawyer born in Philadelphia. He was the first African-American to receive a degree from Harvard.

9. William Dean Howells (1837–1920) was a highly acclaimed writer. His novel *Imperative Duty* (1891) addresses the issue of miscegenation.

of color." This is the height of enlightenment! and from Dean
Howells too, litterateur, diplomat, journalist, altruist!

Art, goodness, and beauty are assaulted in order to stimulate
or apologize for prejudice against the educated Negro!

In Dr. Huguet, we have as a type a man pitifully trying to be
self-conscious, struggling to feel within himself, what prejudice
and custom demand that he feel.

In "A Question of Color" the type is a man of splendid English
training, that of an English gentleman, surrounded from his birth
by wealth, and accepted in the most polished society, married
to a white girl, who sells herself for money, and after the cere-
mony like an angelic Sunday-school child, shudders and admits
the truth, that she can never forget that he is a Negro, and he is
cad enough to say, so says the writer, that he will say his prayers
at her feet night and morning notwithstanding![10]

We all know, no man, negro or other, ever enacted such a part;
it is wholly inconsistent with anything short of a natural-born
idiot! And yet a reputable house offers this trash to the public,
but thanks to a sensible public, it has been received with jeers.
And so stuff like this comes apace, influencing the reading-world,
not indeed thinkers and scholars; but the indiscriminate reading
world, upon whom rests, unfortunately, the bulk of senseless
prejudice.

Conan Doyle, like Howells, also pays his thoughtful attention
to the educated negro—making him in this case more bloodthirsty
and treacherous and savage than the Seminole.[11] One more, and
these are mentioned only to show the kind of types of Negro
characters eminent writers have taken exceeding care to place before the world as representing us.

In the "Condition of Women in the United States," Mme.
Blanc, in a volume of 285 pages, devotes less than 100 words to
negro women; after telling ironically of a "Black Damsel" in New

10. Matthews may be referring to another story or novel addressing
the issue of mixed-blood and the stereotype of the tragic mulatto who
supposedly embodied the worst qualities of both races. The mulatto became one of the most popular characters in American fiction.

11. Sir Arthur Conan Doyle (1859–1930) was an English author who
created the character Sherlock Holmes.

Orleans engaged in teaching Latin, she describes her attire, the arrangement of her hair, and concludes, "I also saw a class of little Negro girls with faces like monkeys studying Greek, and the disgust expressed by their former masters seemed quite justified."

Her knowledge of history is as imperfect so far as veracity goes, as her avowal in the same book of her freedom from prejudice against the Negro. The "little girls" must have been over thirty years old to have had any former masters even at their birth! And all this is the outcome in the nineteenth century of the highest expressions of Anglo-Saxon acumen, criticism and understanding of the powers of Negroes of America!

The point of all this, is the indubitable evidence of the need of thoughtful, well-defined and intelligently placed efforts on our part, to serve as counter-irritants against all such writing that shall stand, having as an aim the supplying of influential and accurate information, on all subjects relating to the Negro and his environments, to inform the American mind at least, for literary purposes.

We cannot afford any more than any other people to be indifferent to the fact, that the surest road to real fame is through literature. Who is so well known and appreciated by the cultured minds as Dumas of France, and Pushkin of Russia? I need not say to this thoughtful and intelligent gathering that, any people without a literature is valued lightly the world round. Who knows or can judge of our intrinsic worth, without actual evidences of our breadth of mind, our boundless humanity. Appearing well and weighted with many degrees of titles, will not raise us in our own estimation while color is the white elephant in America. Yet, America is but a patch on the universe: if she ever produces a race out of her cosmopolitan population, that can look beyond mere money-getting to more permanent qualities of true greatness as a nation, it will call this age her unbalanced stage.

No one thinks of mere color when looking upon the Chinese, but the dignified character of the literature of his race, and he for monotony of expression, color and undesirable individual habits is far inferior in these points to the ever-varying American Negro. So our people must awaken to the fact, that our task is a conquest for a place for ourselves, and is a legitimate ground for action for us, if we shall resolve to conquer it.

While we of to-day view with increasing dissatisfaction the trend of the literary productions of this country, concerning us, yet are we standing squarely on the foundation laid for us by our immediate predecessors?

This is the question I would bring to your minds. Are we adding to the structure planned for us by our pioneers? Do we know our dwelling and those who under many hardships, at least, gathered the material for its upbuilding? Knowing them do we honor—do we love them—what have they done that we should love? Your own Emerson says—"To judge the production of a people you must transplant the spirit of the times in which they lived."

In the ten volumes of American Literature edited by H. L. Stoddard only Phyllis Wheatley and George W. Williams find a place.[12] This does not show that we have done nothing in literature; far from it, but it does show that we have done nothing so brilliant, so effective, so startling as to attract the attention of these editors. Now it is a fact that thoughtful, scholarly white people do not look for literature in its highest sense, from us any more than they look for high scholarship, profound and critical learning on any one point, nor for any eminent judicial acumen or profound insight into causes and effects.

These are properly regarded as the results only of matured intellectual growth or abundant leisure and opportunity, when united with exceptional talents, and this is the world's view, and it is in the main a correct one. Even the instances of precocious geniuses and the rare examples of extraordinary talent appearing from humble and unpromising parentage and unfortuitous surroundings, are always recognized as brilliant, sporadic cases, exceptions.

Consequently our success in Race Literature will be looked upon with curiosity and only a series of projected enterprises in various directions—history, poetry, novel writing, speeches, orations, forensic effort, sermons, and so on, will have the result of gaining for us recognition.

You recall Poteghine's remark in Turgenef's [sic] novel of

12. George W. Williams (1849–1891) wrote about the experiences of blacks during the Civil War and the period between the Jamestown Landing and Reconstruction.

"Smoke."[13] How well it applies to us. "For heaven's sake do not spread the idea in Russia that we can achieve success without preparation. No, if your brow be seven spans in width *study*, begin with the alphabet or *else remain quiet* and say nothing. Oh! it excites me to think of these things."

Dr. Blyden's essays, Dr. Crummell's sermons and addresses, and Professor Greener's orations, all are high specimens of sustained English, good enough for any one to read, and able to bear critical examination, and reflect the highest credit on the race.[14]

Your good city of Boston deserves well for having given us our first real historian, William C. Nell—his history of "The Colored Patriots of the Revolution"—not suffieciently read nowadays or appreciated by the present generation; a scholarly, able, accurate book, second to none written by any other colored man.[15]

William Wells Brown's "Black Man" was a worthy tribute in its day, the precursor of more elaborate books, and should be carefully studied now; his "Sights and Scenes Abroad" was probably the first book of travel written by an American Negro. The same is doubtless true of his novel, "Clotilde."[16] The "Anglo-African" magazine published in New York City in 1859, is adjudged by competent authority to be the highest, best, most scholarly written of all the literature published by us in fifty years.

We have but to read the graphic descriptions and eloquent passages in the first edition of the "Life and Times" of Frederick Douglass to see the high literary qualities of which the race is

13. Ivan Sergeyevich Turgenev (1818–1883) was a Russian author. "Smoke" is a short story included in *The Best Known Works of Ivan Turgenev* (New York: Famous Classics Library, 1942).

14. Edward Wilmot Blyden (1832–1912) was one of the principal spokesmen for Pan-Africanism in the nineteenth century, along with Crummell and Martin R. Delany. He originated the expression "African personality."

15. William C. Nell (1816–1874) was an educator and writer. He wrote *Service of Colored Americans in the Wars of 1775 and 1812* (1852). It was revised in 1855 as *The Colored Patriots of the American Revolution with Sketches of Several Distinguished Colored Persons to Which Is Added a Brief Survey of the Condition and Prospects of Colored Americans.*

16. William Wells Brown (1816–1884) was a historian and novelist. "Clotilde" refers to *Clotel, or the President's Daughter*, which was published in London in 1853 and in the U.S. in 1867.

capable. "Light and Truth," a valuable volume published many
years ago; Dr. Perry's "Cushite!" "Bond and Free, or Under the
Yoke," by John S. Ladue; "The Life of William Lloyd Garrison,"
by Archibald Grimké; Joseph Wilson's "Black Phalanx," and "Men
of Mark," by Rev. W. J. Simmons; "Noted Women," by Dr.
Scruggs; "The Negro Press and Its Editors," by I. Garland Penn;
"Paul Dunbar's Dialect Poems," which have lately received high
praise from the Hoosier Poet, James Whitcomb Reilly, "Johnson's
School History;" "From a Virginia Cabin to the Capitol," by
Hon. J. M. Langston; "Iola Leroy," by Mrs. F. E. W. Harper;
"Music and Some Highly Musical People," by James M. Trotter,
are specimen books within easy reach of the public, that will in-
crease in interest with time.[17]

Professor R. T. Greener as a metaphysician, logician, orator,
and prize essayist, holds an undisputed position in the annals of
our literature second to none. His defense of the Negro in the
"National Quarterly Review," 1880, in reply to Mr. Parton's stric-
tures, has been an arsenal from which many have since supplied
their armor. It was quoted extensively in this country and England.[18]

And it is not generally known that one of the most valuable
contributions to Race Literature, has appeared in the form of a
scientific treatise on "Incandescent Lighting" published by Van
Nostrand of New York, and thus another tribute is laid to Boston's credit by Lewis H. Latimer.

In the ecclesiastical line we have besides those already mentioned, the writings of the learned Dr. Pennington, Bishops Payne
and Tanner of the A.M.E. Church.

The poems, songs and addresses by our veteran literary women
F. E. W. Harper, Charlotte Forten Grimké, H. Cordelia Ray, Gertrude Mossell, "Clarence and Corinne," "The Hazeltone Family"
by Mrs. G. E. Johnson, and "Appointed" by W. H. Stowers, and

17. One good reference for the works cited here is Peter Bergman's
Chronological History of the Negro in America (New York: Harper and
Row, 1969).
18. Greener is commenting on James Parton's "Antipathy to the
Negro" in which Parton asserts that blacks are imitators and not creators
of culture.

W. H. Anderson are a few of the publications on similar subjects; all should be read and placed in our libraries, as first beginnings it is true, but they compare favorably with similar work of the most advanced people.[19]

Our journalism has accomplished more than can now be estimated; in fact not until careful biographers make special studies drawn from the lives of the pioneer journalists, shall we or those contemporary with them ever know the actual meed of good work accomplished by them under almost insurmountable difficulties.

Beginning with the editors of the first newspapers published in this country by colored men, we New Yorkers take pride in the fact that Messrs. Cornish and Russwurm of "Freedom's Journal," New York City, 1827, edited the first paper in this country devoted to the upbuilding of the Negro. Philip A. Bell of the "Weekly Advocate," 1837, was named by contemporaries "the Nestor of African American journalists." The gifted Dr. James McCune Smith was associated with him. The "Weekly Advocate" later became the "Colored American." And in 1839, on Mr. Bell's retirement Dr. Charles Ray assumed the editorial chair, continued until 1842, making an enviable record for zeal on all matters of race interest. These men were in very truth the Pioneers of Race Journalism.

Their lives and record should be zealously guarded for the future use of our children, for they familiarized the public with the idea of the Negro owning and doing the brain work of a newspaper. The people of other sections became active in establishing journals, which did good work all along the line. Even the superficial mind must accept the modest claim that "These journals proved a powerful lever in diverting public opinion, public sympathy, and public support towards the liberation of the slave."

Papers were edited by such men as Dr. H. H. Garnet, David Ruggles, W. A. Hodges and T. Van Rensselaer, of the "Ram's Horn." In 1847 our beloved and lofty minded Frederick Douglass

19. For further reference and explanation of names and accomplishments see Davis's *Contribution of Black Women to America*, vol. 1; Bergman's *Chronological History of the Negro in America*; Plosky and William's *The Negro Almanac*; and Shockley's *Afro-American Women Writers 1746–1933*.

edited his own paper "The North Star," in the City of Rochester, where his mortal remains now peacefully rest. His paper was
noted for its high class matter—and it had the effect of raising the
plane of journalism thereafter. About this time Samuel Ringold
Ward of the "Impartial Citizen," published in Syracuse, N.Y.,
"forged to the front," winning in after years from Mr. Douglass
a most flattering tribute. "Samuel Ringold Ward," the sage of
Anacostia once said to the writer, "was one of the smartest men
I ever knew if not the smartest."

The prevailing sentiment at that time was sympathy for the ambitious Negro. At a most opportune time, "The Anglo African,"
the finest effort in the way of a newspaper made by the race up
to that time, was established in January of 1859 in New York City,
with Thomas Hamilton as editor and proprietor. The columns
were opened to the most experienced writers of the day. Martin
R. Delaney contributed many important papers on astronomy,
among which was one on "Comets," another on "The Attraction
of the Planets." George B. Vashon wrote "The Successive Advances of Astronomy," James McCune Smith wrote his comments "On the Fourteenth Query of Thomas Jefferson's Notes
on Virginia" and his "German Invasion"—every number contained gems that to-day are beyond price. In these pages also appeared "Afric-American Picture Gallery," by "Ethiope"—Wm.
J. Wilson; Robert Gordon's "Personality of the First Cause;" Dr.
Pennington on "The Self-Redeeming Power of the Colored Races
of the World;" Dr. Blyden on "The Slave Traffic;" and on the
current questions of the day, such brave minds as Frederick Douglass, William C. Nell, John Mercer Langston, Theodore Holly, J.
Sella Martin, Frances Ellen Watkins, Jane Rustic, Sarah M. Douglass, and Grace A. Mapps! What a galaxy! The result was a genu-
ine race newspaper, one that had the courage to eliminate everything of personal interest, and battle for the rights of the whole
people, and while its history, like many other laudable enterprises,
may be little known beyond the journalistic fraternity, to such
men as Wendell Phillips and William Lloyd Garrison, the paper
and staff were well known and appreciated.[20] In those days, the

20. Most of these writers dealt with race or abolition issues. They
were also well known for their contributions in other areas.

Negro in literature was looked upon as a prodigy; he was encouraged in many ways by white people particularly, as he was useful in serving the cause of philanthropic agitators for the liberation of the slave. The earnest, upright character and thoughtful minds of the early pioneers acted as a standing argument in favor of the cause for which the abolitionists were then bending every nerve when the slave was liberated and the Civil War brought to a close. The spirit of Mr. Lincoln's interview with a committee of colored citizens of the District of Columbia, in August, 1862, as told by William Wells Brown, in which Mr. Lincoln said, "But for your people among us, there would be no war," reacted upon the public, and from that time until the present, a vigorous system of oppression, under the name of natural prejudice, has succeeded immeasurably in retarding our progress.

As a matter of history, we have nothing to compare with the weekly publications of 25 or 30 years ago. The unequal contest waged between Negro journals and their white contemporaries is lost sight of by the people, as only those connected with various publications are aware of the condition and difficulties surrounding the managements of such journals.

Our struggling journalists not only find themselves on the losing side, but as if to add to their thankless labor, they oftentimes receive the contemptuous regard of the people who should enthusiastically rally to their support. The journalist is spurred with the common sense idea that every enterprise undertaken and carried on by members of the race is making a point in history for that entire race, and the historians of the future will not stop to consider our discontented and sentimental whys and wherefores, when they critically examine our race enterprises; but they will simply record their estimate of what the men and women journalists of to-day not only represented, but actually accomplished.

It is so often claimed that colored newspapers do not amount to anything. People even who boast of superior attainments, voice such sentiments with the most ill-placed indifference; the most discreditable phase of race disloyalty imaginable—one that future historians will have no alternative but to censure.

If our newspapers and magazines do not amount to anything, it is because our people do not demand anything of better quality from their own. It is because they strain their purses supporting those white papers that are and always will be independent of any income derived from us. Our contributions to such journals are spasmodic and uncertain, like fluctuating stocks, and are but an excess of surplus. It is hard for the bulk of our people to see this; it is even hard to prove to them that in supporting such journals, published by the dominant class, we often pay for what are not only vehicles of insult to our manhood and womanhood, but we assist in propagating or supporting false impressions of ourselves or our less fortunate brothers.

Our journalistic leader is unquestionably T. Thomas Fortune, Editor of "The New York Age," and a regular contributor of signed articles to the "New York Sun," one of the oldest and ablest daily newspapers in the United States, noted on two continents for its rare excellence.

For many years Mr. Fortune has given his best efforts to the cause of race advancement, and the splendid opportunities now opening to him on the great journals of the day, attest the esteem in which he is held by men who create public opinion in this country.

If John E. Bruce, "Bruce-Grit," "John Mitchell, Jr." W. H. A. Moore, Augustus M. Hodge "B Square," were members of any other race, they would be famous the country over. Joe Howard or "Bill Nye" have in reality done no more for their respective clientage than these bright minds and corresponding wits have done for theirs.

T. T. Fortune of "The Age," Ida Wells-Barnet[t] of the "Free Speech," and John Mitchell of the "Richmond Planet," have made a nobler fight than the brilliant Parnell in his championship of Ireland's cause, for the reason that the people for whom he battled, better knew and utilized more the strength obtained only by systematic organization, not so is the case with the constituents of the distinguished journalists I have mentioned. [21]

Depressing as this fact is, it should not deter those who know

21. Timothy Thomas Fortune (1856–1928) was a newspaper editor and writer. He formed the Afro-American League, which worked for the full rights of African-Americans, and he established the Washington *Sun*. For further explanation on others mentioned, refer to materials on the black press. For more information on Ida Wells, see Davis's *Contributions of Black Women to America*, vol. 1.

that Race Literature should be cultivated for the sake of the formation of habits. First efforts are always crude, each succeeding one becomes better or should be so. Each generation by the law of heredity receives the impulse or impression for good or ill from its predecessors, and since this is the law, we must begin to form habits of observation and commence to build a plan for posterity by synthesis, analysis, ourselves aiming and striving after the highest, whether we attain it or not. Such are the attempts of our journalists of to-day, and they shall reap if they faint not.

Race Literature does not mean things uttered in praise, thoughtless praise of ourselves, wherein each goose thinks her gosling a swan. We have had too much of this, too much that is crude, rude, pompous, and literary nothings, which ought to have been strangled before they were written much less printed; and this does not only apply to us; for it is safe to say that, only an infinitesimal percentage of the so-called literature filling the book shelves to-day, will survive a half century.

In the words of a distinguished critic, "It is simply amazing" how little of all that is written and printed in these days that makes for literature; how small a part is permanent, how much purely ephemeral, famous to-day on account of judicious advertising, forgotten tomorrow. We should clear away the under-brush of self-deception which makes the novice think because sentences are strung together and ordinary ideas evolved, dilated upon and printed, that such trash is literature." If this is claimed for the more favored class, it should have a tendency with us to encourage our work, even though the results do not appear at once.

It should serve the student by guarding him against the fulsome praise of "great men," "great writers," "great lawyers," "great ministers," who in reality have never done one really great or meritorious thing.

Rather should the student contemplate the success of such as Prof. DuBois who won the traveling fellowship at Harvard on metaphysical studies, and has just received his Ph.D., at the last commencement, on account of his work. For such facts demonstrate that it is the character of the work we do, rather than the quantity of it, which counts for real Race Literature.

Race Literature does mean though the preserving of all the rec-

ords of a Race, and thus cherishing the materials saving from destruction and obliteration what is good, helpful and stimulating.
But for our Race Literature, how will future generations know
of the pioneers in Literature, our statesmen, soldiers, divines, mu-
sicians, artists, lawyers, critics, and scholars? True culture in Race
Literature will enable us to discriminate and not to write hasty
thoughts and unjust and ungenerous criticism often of our supe-
riors in knowledge and judgment.

And now comes the question, What part shall we women play
in the Race Literature of the future? I shall best answer that question by calling your attention to the glorious part which they have
already performed in the columns of the "Woman's Era," edited
by Josephine St. P. Ruffin.

Here within the compass of one small journal we have struck
out a new line of departure—a journal, a record of Race interests
gathered from all parts of the United States, carefully selected,
moistened, winnowed and garnered by the ablest intellects of educated colored women, shrinking at no lofty theme, shirking no
serious duty, aiming at every possible excellence, and determined
to do their part in the future uplifting of the race.

If twenty women, by their concentrated efforts in one literary movement, can meet with such success as has engendered,
planned out, and so successfully consummated this convention,
what much more glorious results, what wider spread success, what
grander diffusion of mental light will not come forth at the bidding of the enlarged hosts of women writers, already called into
being by the stimulus of your efforts?

And here let me speak one word for my journalistic sisters who
have already entered the broad arena of journalism. Before the
"Woman's Era" had come into existence, no one except themselves can appreciate the bitter experience and sore disappoint-
ments under which they have at all times been compelled to pursue their chosen vocations.

If their brothers of the press have had their difficulties to contend with, I am here as a sister journalist to state, from the fullness
of knowledge, that their task has been an easy one compared with
that of the colored woman in journalism.

Woman's part in Race Literature, as in Race building, is the most important part and has been so in all ages. It is for her to receive impressions and transmit them. All through the most remote epochs she has done her share in literature. When not an active singer like Sappho, she has been the means of producing poets, statesmen, and historians, understandingly as Napoleon's mother worked on Homeric tapestry while bearing the future conqueror of the world.

When living up to her highest development, woman has done much to make lasting history, by her stimulating influence and there can be no greater responsibility than that, and this is the highest privilege granted to her by the Creator of the Universe.

Such are some brief outlines of the vast problem of Race Literature. Never was the outlook for Race Literature brighter. Questions of vast importance to succeeding generations on all lines are now looming up to be dissected and elucidated.

Among the students of the occult, certain powers are said to be fully developed innately in certain types of the Negro, powers that when understood and properly directed will rival if not transcend those of Du Maurier's Svengali.[22]

The medical world recognizes this especially when investigating the science of neurology,—by the merest chance it was discovered that certain types of our nurses—male and female—possessed invaluable qualities for quieting and controlling patients afflicted with the self-destructive mania. This should lead our physicians to explore and investigate so promising a field.

American artists find it easy to caricature the Negro, but find themselves baffled when striving to depict the highest characteristics of a Sojourner Truth. If he lacks the required temperament, there is thus offered a field for the race-loving Negro artist to compete with his elder brother in art, and succeed where the other has failed.

American and even European historians have often proved them-

22. Du Maurier's Svengali refers to a person who completely overpowers another, based on George Du Maurier's myth of a student who had the mesmeric spell of evil hypnotist Svengali placed on her so that when he died her voice died and she was unable to continue her talent for singing.

selves much enchained by narrow local prejudice, hence there is a field for the unbiased historian of this closing century.

The advance made during the last fifteen or twenty years in mechanical science is of the most encouraging nature possible for our own ever-increasing class of scientific students.

The scholars of the race, linguists and masters of the dead languages have a wide field before them, which when fully explored, will be of incalculable interest to the whole people—I mean particularly the translators of the writings of the ancient world, on all that pertains to the exact estimate in which our African ancestors were held by contemporaries. This will be of interest to all classes, and especially to our own.

Until our scholars shall apply themselves to these greatly neglected fields, we must accept the perverted and indifferent translations of those prejudiced against us.

Dr. Le Plongeon, an eminent explorer and archaeologist, in his Central American studies, has made startling discoveries, which, if he succeeds in proving, will mean that the cradle of man's primitive condition is situated in Yucatan, and the primitive race was the ancestor of the Negro.

The "Review of Reviews," of July has this to say: "That such a tradition should have been handed down to the modern Negro is not so improbable in view of the fact that the inhabitants of Africa appear certainly to have had communication with the people of the Western world up to the destruction of the Island of Atlanta, concerning which events Dr. Le Plongeon has much to tell us."

Think of it! What a scope for our scholars not only in archaeology, but in everything that goes to make up literature!

Another avenue of research that commands dignified attention is the possibility that Negroes were among those who embarked with Columbus. Prominent educators are giving serious attention to this. Prof. Wright, of Georgia, lately sailed to England with the express purpose of investigating the subject, during his vacation, in some of the famous old libraries of Europe.

The lesson to be drawn from this cursory glance at what I may call the past, present and future of our Race Literature, apart from its value as first beginnings, not only to us as a people but literature in general, is that unless earnest and systematic effort be made to procure and preserve for transmission to our successors, the records, books and various publications already produced by us, not only will the sturdy pioneers who paved the way and laid the foundation for our Race Literature, be robbed of their just due, but an irretrievable wrong will be inflicted upon the generations that shall come after us.

THE AWAKENING OF THE AFRO-AMERICAN WOMAN
(1897)

THE AWAKENING TO LIFE OF ANY OF THE FORCES OF NATURE IS THE most mysterious as it is the sublimest of spectacles. Through all nature there runs a thread of life. We watch with equal interest and awe the transformation of the rosebud into the flower and the babe into manhood. The philosopher has well said that the element of life runs through all nature and links the destinies of earth with the destinies of the stars. This is a beautiful and ennobling thought; while it binds to earth it yet lifts us to heaven. It gives us strength in adversity, when the storms beat and the thunders peal forth their diapason and confusion reigns supreme everywhere; it tempers our joys with soberness when prosperity hedges us about as the dews of the morning hedge about with gladness the modest violet shyly concealed by the wayside. Life is the most mysterious as it is the most revealed force in nature. Death does not compare with it in these qualities, for there can be no death without life. It is from this point of view that we must regard the tremendous awakening of the Afro-American womanhood, during the past three decades from the double night of ages of slavery in which it was locked in intellectual and moral eclipse. It has been the awakening of a race from the nightmare of 250 years of self-effacement and debasement. It is not within the power of any one who has stood outside of Afro-American life to adequately estimate the extent of the effacement and debasement, and, therefore, of the gracious awakening which has quickened into life the slumbering forces and filled with hope and gladness the souls of millions of the womanhood of our land. To the God of love and tenderness and pity and justice we ascribe the fullness of our thanks and prayers for the transformation from the death of slavery to the life of freedom. All the more are we grateful to the moral and Christian forces of the world, the Christian statesmen and soldiers and scholars who were the divine instruments who

Published with the permission of the Yale Collection of American Literature, Beinecke Rare Book and Manuscript Library, Yale University.

made it possible for this womanhood to stand in this august presence to-day, this vast army laboring for the upbuilding of the
Master's kingdom among men; for it is true as Longfellow said:

> Were half the power that fills the world with terror,
> Were half the wealth bestowed on camps and courts,
> Given to redeem the human mind from error,
> There were no need of arsenals and forts.

The auction block of brutality has been changed into the forum
of reason, the slave mart has been replaced by the schoolroom and
the church.

As I stand here to-day clothed in the garments of Christian
womanhood, the horrible days of slavery, out of which I came,
seem as a dream that is told, some horror incredible. Indeed, could
they have been, and are not? They were; they are not; this is the
sum and substance, the shame and the glory of the tale that I would
tell, of the message that I would bring.

In the vast economy of nature, cycles of time are of small moment, years are as hours, and seconds bear but small relation to
the problem, yet they are as the drops of rain that fall to earth and
lodge in the fastnesses of the mountain from which our rivers are
formed that feed the vast expanse of ocean. So in the history of
a race lifting itself out of its original condition of helplessness,
time is as necessary an element as is opportunity, in the assisting
forces of humankind.

When we remember that the God who created all things is no
respecter [*sic*] of persons, that the black child is beloved of Him
as the white child, we can more easily fix the responsibility that
rests upon the Christian womanhood of the country to join with
us in elevating the head, the heart and the soul of Afro-American
womanhood. As the great Frederick Douglass once said, in order
to measure the heights to which we have risen we must first measure the depths to which we were dragged. It is from this point
of observation that we must regard the awakening of the Afro-
American womanhood of the land. And what is this awakening?
What is its distinguishing characteristics? It would seem super-
fluous to ask or to answer questions so obvious, but the lamen-

table truth is, that the womanhood of the United States, of the world, knows almost absolutely nothing of the hope and aspirations, of the joys and the sorrows, of the wrongs, and of the needs of the black women of this country, who came up out of the effacement and debasement of American slavery into the dazzling sunlight of freedom. My friends, call to mind the sensations of the prisoner of Chillon, as he walked out of the dungeon where the flower of his life had been spent, into the open air, and you will be able to appreciate in some sense our feelings in 1865,

When the war drums throbbed no longer,
And the battle flags were furled.

What a past was ours! There was no attribute of womanhood which had not been sullied—aye, which had not been despoiled in the crucible of slavery. Virtue, modesty, the joys of maternity, even hope of mortality, all those were the heritage of this womanhood when the voice of Lincoln and the sword of Grant, as the expression of the Christian opinion of the land, bade them stand forth, without let or hindrance, as arbiters of their own persons and wills. They had no past to which they could appeal for anything. It had destroyed, more than in the men, all that a woman holds sacred, all that ennobles womanhood. She had but the future.

From such small beginnings she was compelled to construct a home. She who had been an outcast, the caprice of brutal power and passion, who had been educated to believe that morality was an echo, and womanly modesty a name; she who had seen father and brother and child torn from her and hurried away into everlasting separation—this creature was born to life in an hour and expected to create a home.

Home, sweet home;
Be it ever so humble,
There's no place like home.

My friends, more, home is the noblest, the most sacred spot in a Christian nation. It is the foundation upon which nationality rests, the pride of the citizen and the glory of the Republic. This woman was expected to build a home for 4,500,000 people, of whom she was the decisive unit. No Spartan mother ever had a larger task imposed upon her shoulders; no Spartan mother ever acquitted herself more heroically than this Afro-American woman has done. She has done it almost without any assistance from her white sister; who, in too large a sense, has left her to work out her own destiny in fear and trembling. The color of the skin has been an almost insurmountable barrier between them, despite the beautiful lines of the gentle Cowper, that—

Skin may differ,
But affection
Dwells in black and white the same.

I am not unmindful, however, of the Northern women who went into the South after the war as the missionary goes into the dark places of the world, and helped the Afro-American women to lay the foundation of her home broad and deep in the Christian virtues. For years they did this in the schoolroom and their labors naturally had their reflex in the home life of their pupils.

Broadly speaking, my main statement holds, however, that these women, starting empty handed, were left to make Christian homes where a Christian citizenship should be nurtured. The marvel is not that they have succeeded, not that they are succeeding, but that they did not fail, *utterly fail*. I believe the God who brought them out of the Valley of the Shadow, who snatched them from the hand of the white rapist, the base slave master whose unacknowledged children are to be found in every hamlet of the Republic, guided these women, and guides them in the supreme work of building their Christian homes. The horrors of the past were forgotten in the joyous labor that presented itself. Even the ineffaceable wrongs of the past, while not forgotten, were forgiven in the spirit of the Master, who even forgave those who took His life.

If there had been no other awakening than this, if this woman who had stood upon the auction block possessed of no rights that a white man was bound to respect, and none which he did respect, if there had been no other awakening of the Afro-American woman than this, that she made a home for her race, an abiding place for husband, and son, and daughter, it would be glory enough to embalm her memory in song and story. As it is, it will be her sufficient monument through all time that out of nothing she created something, and that something the dearest, the sweetest, the strongest institution in Christian government.

But she has done more than this. The creation of a home is the central feature of her awakening, but around this are many other features which show her strong title to the countenance and respect of the sisterhood of the world. She has meekly taken her place by her husband, in the humble occupations of life as a bread winner, and by her labors and sacrifices has helped to rear and educate 50,000 young women, who are active instructors in the Christian churches of the land. In the building up of the Master's kingdom she has been and she is an active and a positive influence; indeed, in this field she has proven, as her white sister has proven, the truth of Napoleon Bonaparte's sententious but axiomatic truth, that "The hand that rocks the cradle rules the world." It is not too much to say that the 7,000,000 Afro-American church memberships would fall to pieces as a rope of sand if the active sympathy and support of the Afro-American women were withdrawn. It is demonstrable that these women are the arch of the Afro-American temple. But these women who came out of slavery have done more than this. They have not only made Christian homes for their families, and educated 50,000 Sunday-school workers, but they have given to the State 25,000 educated school teachers, who are to-day the hope and inspiration of the whole race. The black women who came out of slavery in the past thirty years, have accomplished these tremendous results as farm-laborers and house servants, and they deserve the admiration of mankind for the glorious work that they have accomplished. In the past few years the educated daughters of these ex-slave women have aroused themselves to the necessity of systematic organization for their own protection, and for strengthening their race where they find it is weak, and to this end they have in the several States 243 regularly organized and officered clubs in the Afro-American Women's National Association; there are besides hundreds of social clubs and temperance organizations working in their own way for a strong Christian womanhood. Indeed, the impulse of aspiration after the strong and the good in our civilization is manifest on all hands in our womanhood. It is all so grounded in Christian morality that we may safely conclude that it is built upon a rock and cannot be shaken by the fury of the storms.

The awakening of the Afro-American woman is one of the most promising facts in our national life. That she deserves the active sympathy and co-operation of all the female forces of the Republic, I think I have sufficiently shown. We need them. We have always needed them. We need them in the work of religion, of education, of temperance, of morality, of industrialism; and above all we need their assistance in combatting the public opinion and laws that degrade our womanhood because it is black and not white; for of a truth, and as a universal law, an injury to one woman is an injury to all women. As long as the affections are controlled by legislation in defiance of Christian law, making infamous the union of black and white, we shall have unions without the sanction of the law, and children without legal parentage, to the degradation of black womanhood and the disgrace of white manhood. As one woman, as an Afro-American woman, I stand in this great Christian presence to-day and plead that the marriage and divorce laws be made uniform throughout the Republic, and that they shall not control, but legalize, the union of mutual affections. Until this shall have been done, Afro-American womanhood will have known no full and absolute awakening. As the laws now stand, they are the greatest demoralizing forces with which our womanhood has to contend. They serve as the protection of the white man, but they leave us defenceless, indeed. I ask the Christian womanhood of this great organized Army of Christ, to lend us their active co-operation in coercing the lawmakers of the land in throwing around our womanhood the equal protection of the State to which it is entitled. A slave regulation should not be allowed to prevail in a free government. A barbarous injustice should not receive the sanction of a Christian nation. The stronger forces of society should scorn to crush to the earth one of the weakest forces.

Next to these degrading marriage and divorce laws which prevail in two [sic] many States of the Republic, the full awakening
of the Afro-American woman to her rightful position in society,
are the separate car regulations which prevail in most of the States
of the South. They were conceived in injustice; they are executed
with extraordinary cowardice. Their entire operation tends to degrade Afro-American womanhood. None who are familiar with
their operation will dispute this statement of facts. From this ex-
alted forum, and in the name of the large army of Afro-American
women, I appeal to the Christian sentiment which dominates this
organization, to assist us in righting the wrongs growing out of
these regulations, to the end that our womanhood may be sustained in its dignity and protected in its weakness, and the heav-
enly Father, who hath declared, "righteousness exalteth a nation,
but sin is a reproach to any people," will give His benediction to
the laws made just.

I am moved here further to invoke your patience and sympathy
in the efforts of our awakening womanhood to care for the aged
and infirm, for the orphan and outcast; for the reformation of the
penal institutions of the Southern States, for the separation of
male and female convicts, and above all for the establishment of
juvenile reformatories [in] those States for both races, to the end
that the shame of it may be removed that children of tender age
should be herded with hardened criminals from whose life all of
moral sensibility has vanished forever.

I feel moved to speak here in this wise for a whole race of
women whose rise or fall, whose happiness or sorrow, whose degradation or exaltation are the concern of Christian men and women
everywhere. I feel moved to say in conclusion that in all Christian
and temperance work, in all that lifts humanity from its fallen
condition to a more perfect resemblance of Him in whose image
it was made, in all that goes to make our common humanity
stronger and better and more beautiful; the Afro-American women
of the Republic will "do their duty as God shall give them light
to do it."

References
Index

REFERENCES

SOURCES OF SPEECHES

MARIA W. STEWART (1803–1879)

Lecture Delivered at the Franklin Hall
  Stewart, Maria W. *Productions of Mrs. Maria Stewart, Presented to the First African Baptist Church and Society, in the City of Boston.* Boston: Friends of Freedom and Virtue, 1835. Reprinted in *Spiritual Narratives*, edited by Henry Louis Gates. New York: Oxford University Press, 1988, pp. 51–56.

An Address Delivered Before the Afric-American Female Intelligence Society of Boston
  Stewart, Maria W. *Productions of Mrs. Maria Stewart, Presented to the First African Baptist Church and Society, in the City of Boston.* Boston: Friends of Freedom and Virtue, 1835. Reprinted in *Spiritual Narratives*, edited by Henry Louis Gates. New York: Oxford University Press, 1988, pp. 56–63.

SOJOURNER TRUTH (c. 1797–1883)

Speech Delivered to the Woman's Rights Convention, Akron, Ohio
  Gage Version: Truth, Sojourner. *Narrative of Sojourner Truth.* With Olive Gilbert, 1850; revised by Frances W. Titus, 1875, 1884. Reprint. Salem, NH: Ayer, 1988, pp. 133–135.
  Campbell Version: Campbell, Karlyn Kohrs. *Key Texts of the Early Feminists.* Vol. 2 of *Man Cannot Speak for Her.* Westport, CT: Greenwood Press, 1989, pp. 100–101.

Speech Delivered to the First Annual Meeting of the American Equal Rights Association
  Stanton, Elizabeth, Susan B. Anthony, and Matilda J. Gage, eds. *History of Woman Suffrage*, vol. 2 (1861–1876). Rochester, NY: Charles Mann, 1881. Reprint. New York: Source Book Press, 1970, pp. 193–194.

FRANCES ELLEN WATKINS HARPER (1825–1911)

"Duty to Dependent Races"
  Avery, Rachel Foster, ed. *Transactions of the National Council of Women of the United States.* Philadelphia: J. B. Lippincott, 1891, pp. 86–91.

"Woman's Political Future"
  Sewall, May Wright. *The World's Congress of Representative Women.* Chicago: Rand, McNally & Company, 1894, pp. 433–437.

ANNA JULIA HAYWOOD COOPER (1858–1964)

"Womanhood a Vital Element in the Regeneration and Progress of a Race"
Cooper, Anna Julia. *A Voice from the South by a Black Woman of the South*. Xenia, OH: Aldine Printing House, 1892. Reprint. New York: Oxford University Press, 1988, pp. 9–47.

IDA B. WELLS (1862–1931)

"Lynch Law in All Its Phases"
Our Day: A Record and Review of Current Reform 11 (January–June 1893): 333–347.

FANNIE BARRIER WILLIAMS (1855–1944)

"The Intellectual Progress of the Colored Women of the United States since the Emancipation Proclamation"
Sewall, May Wright. *The World's Congress of Representative Women*. Chicago: Rand, McNally & Company, 1894, pp. 696–711.

VICTORIA EARLE MATTHEWS (1861–1907)

"The Value of Race Literature: An Address Delivered at the First Congress of Colored Women of the United States"
Moorland-Spingarn Research Center, Howard University.

"The Awakening of the Afro-American Woman"
Yale Collection of American Literature, Beinecke Rare Book and Manuscript Library, Yale University.

WORKS CITED

Aristotle. *The Rhetoric and the Poetics of Aristotle*. Modern Library. New York: Random House, 1954.

Avery, Rachel Foster, ed. *Transactions of the National Council of Women of the United States*. Philadelphia: J. B. Lippincott, 1891.

Bennett, Lerone, Jr., *Before the Mayflower: A History of Black America* New York: Penguin, 1984.

Bernard, Jacqueline. *Journey Toward Freedom: The Story of Sojourner Truth*. 1967. Reprint. New York: The Feminist Press, 1990.

Brown, Hallie Q. *Homespun Heroines and Other Women of Distinction*. Xenia, OH: Aldine, 1926.

Campbell, Karlyn Kohrs. *A Critical Study of Early Feminist Rhetoric*. Vol. 1 of *Man Cannot Speak for Her*. Westport, CT: Greenwood Press, 1989.

————. *Key Texts of the Early Feminists.* Vol. 2 of *Man Cannot Speak for Her.* Westport, CT: Greenwood Press, 1989.

Carby, Hazel V. *Reconstructing Womanhood: The Emergence of the Afro-American Woman Novelist.* New York: Oxford University Press, 1987.

Chalmers, Thomas. *The Juvenile Revival; or The Philosophy of the Christian Endeavor Movement.* St. Louis: Christian Publishing Co., 1893.

Davis, Angela Y. *Women, Race, and Class.* 1981. Reprint. New York: Random House, 1983.

Davis, Elizabeth L. *Lifting as They Climb: The National Association of Colored Women.* Washington, DC: National Association of Colored Women, 1933.

DuBois, Ellen Carol. *Feminism and Suffrage: The Emergence of an Independent Women's Movement in America 1848–1869.* Ithaca, NY: Cornell University Press, 1978.

Foner, Philip S., ed. *The Voice of Black America: Major Speeches by Negroes in the United States, 1797–1971.* New York: Simon & Schuster, 1972.

Foster, Frances Smith, ed. *A Brighter Coming Day: A Frances Ellen Watkins Harper Reader.* New York: The Feminist Press, 1990.

Giddings, Paula. *When and Where I Enter: The Impact of Black Women on Race and Sex in America.* New York: Bantam Books, 1984.

Haraway, Donna. "Ecce Homo, Ain't (Ar'n't) I a Woman, and Inappropriate/d Others: The Human in a Post-Humanist Landscape." In *Feminists Theorize the Political*, edited by Judith Butler and Joan W. Scott. New York: Routledge, 1992.

Harley, Sharon. "Anna J. Cooper: A Voice for Black Women." In *The Afro-American Woman: Struggles and Images*, edited by Sharon Harley and Rosalyn Terborg-Penn. Port Washington, NY: Kennikat, 1978.

Harper, Frances W. "We Are All Bound Up Together." In *Proceedings of the Eleventh National Woman's Rights Convention.* Rochester, NY: A. Strong & Company, 1866.

Hutchinson, Louise Daniel. *Anna J. Cooper: A Voice from the South.* Washington, DC: Smithsonian Institution Press, 1981.

Joseph, Gloria I. "Sojourner Truth: Archetypal Black Feminist." In *Wild Women in the Whirlwind: Afra-American Culture and the Contemporary Literary Renaissance*, edited by Joanne M. Braxton and Andree Nicola McLaughlin, 35–47. New Brunswick, NJ: Rutgers University Press, 1990.

Kraditor, Aileen. *The Ideas of the Woman Suffrage Movement, 1899–1929.* Garden City, NY: Doubleday, 1971.

Loewenberg, Bert J., and Ruth Bogin. *Black Women in Nineteenth-Century American Life: Their Words, Their Thoughts, Their Feelings.* University Park and London: Pennsylvania State University Press, 1976.

Lowe, Berenice. "The Family of Sojourner Truth." *Michigan Heritage* 3 (Summer 1962): 181–185.

Mabee, Carleton. "Sojourner Truth, Bold Prophet: Why Did She Never Learn to Read?" *New York History* (January 1988): 55–77.

Malloch, James M. *A Practical Church Dictionary.* New York: Morehouse-Barlow Co., 1964.

Moses, Wilson Jeremiah. *Alexander Crummell: A Study of Civilization and Discontent.* New York: Oxford Press, 1989.

Mossell, Gertrude. *The Work of the Afro-American Woman.* 1894. Reprint. New York: Oxford Press, 1988.

O'Connor, Lillian. *Pioneer Women Orators: Rhetoric in the Ante-Bellum Reform Movement.* New York: Columbia University Press, 1954.

Painter, Nell Irvin. "Sojourner Truth in Life and Memory: Writing the Biography of an American Exotic." *Gender and History* 2 (Spring 1990): 3–16.

Patten, Neil. "The Nineteenth-Century Black Woman as Social Reformer: The 'New' Speeches of Sojourner Truth." *Negro History Bulletin* 49 (January–March 1989): 2–4.

Pointer, Steven R. "Joseph Cook—Apologetics and Science." *Journal of Presbyterian History* 63 (1988): 299–308.

Richardson, Marilyn, ed. *Maria W. Stewart, America's First Black Woman Political Writer: Essays and Speeches.* Bloomington: Indiana University Press, 1987.

Sewall, May Wright. *The World's Congress of Representative Women.* Chicago: Rand, McNally & Company, 1894.

Shockley, Ann Allen. *Afro-American Women Writers 1746–1933: An Anthology and Critical Guide.* New York: New American Library, 1989.

Spear, Allan H. *Black Chicago: The Making of a Negro Ghetto 1890–1920.* Chicago: University of Chicago Press, 1967.

Stanton, Elizabeth, Susan B. Anthony, and Matilda J. Gage, eds. *History of Woman Suffrage,* vol. 2 (1861–1876). Rochester, NY: Charles Mann, 1881. Reprint. New York: Source Book Press, 1970.

Sterling, Dorothy, ed. *We Are Your Sisters: Black Women in the Nineteenth Century.* New York: Norton, 1984.

Stewart, Maria W. *Productions of Mrs. Maria Stewart, Presented to the First African Baptist Church and Society, in the City of Boston.* Boston: Friends of Freedom and Virtue, 1835. Reprinted in *Spiritual Narratives,* edited by Henry Louis Gates. New York: Oxford University Press, 1988.

Still, William. *The Underground Rail Road.* Philadelphia: Porter & Coates, 1872.

Stowe, Harriet Beecher. "Sojourner Truth, the Libyan Sibyl." *Atlantic Monthly* (April 1863): 473–481.

Terry, Esther. "Sojourner Truth: The Person Behind the Libyan Sibyl." *The Massachusetts Review* (Summer–Autumn 1985): 424–444.

Truth, Sojourner. *Narrative of Sojourner Truth.* With Olive Gilbert, 1850;

revised by Frances W. Titus, 1875, 1884. Reprint. Salem, NH: Ayer, 1988.

Washington, Mary Helen. Introduction to *A Voice from the South,* by Anna J. Cooper. New York: Oxford University Press, 1988.

Wells, Ida B. *Crusade for Justice: The Autobiography of Ida B. Wells.* Edited by Alfreda Duster. Chicago: University of Chicago Press, 1970.

Wells-Barnett, Ida. "A Red Record." 1895. Reprinted in *On Lynchings: Southern Horrors, a Red Record, Mob Rule in New Orleans,* 1–101. Reprint. Salem, NH: Ayer, 1990.

———. "Southern Horrors: Lynch Law in All Its Phases." 1892. Reprinted in *On Lynchings: Southern Horrors, a Red Record, Mob Rule in New Orleans,* 4–24. Reprint. Salem, NH: Ayer, 1990.

Wesley, Charles H. *The History of the National Association of Colored Women's Clubs: A Legacy of Service.* Washington, DC: NACW, 1984.

Williams, Fannie B. "A Northern Negro's Autobiography." In *Bearing Witness: Selections from African-American Autobiography in the Twentieth Century,* edited by Henry Louis Gates, 11–22. New York: Pantheon, 1991.

Yellin, Jean Fagan. *Women and Sisters: The Antislavery Feminists in American Culture.* New Haven, CT: Yale University Press, 1989.

INDEX

SHIRLEY WILSON LOGAN, assistant professor of English, directs the Professional Writing Program at the University of Maryland at College Park. She has taught courses in advanced composition, technical writing, the history and practice of rhetoric, and African-American literature. Her published works include articles on the applications of computers to the teaching of writing and on Frances Ellen Watkins Harper and Ida B. Wells. She has written a chapter for *Nineteenth-Century Women Learn to Write* (in press). She is currently working on a study of rhetorical practices among nineteenth- and twentieth-century African-Americans.